'Yeck! What is this glop, Nana?' Sharon listened from behind the garage door to the dinner gaggle in the kitchen. Her kids were grumbling about the chicken salad that Sharon's mother was trying to coerce them into eating. *'It's great. Just try it, you'll see.'* The left over chicken was supposed to tide them over for one extra meal. *'Time for this tired Mom and breadwinner,'* Sharon thought, *'to finish up with the lawn mower repair and go inside to help out.'*

Sharon is a single mother with two children, ages 6 and 9. She has a high school education and spent a year in college before she had to drop out. She works as a clerk/receptionist in a local real estate office and makes $9.50 an hour. She has a second job weekends at a fast food restaurant. Sharon is lucky to have her mother nearby who often can care for the kids. However, she is struggling to make ends meet and thinks maybe she will never really be able to support herself and her children.

> Last week, Sharon took the lawn mower apart, bought some new parts and has just finished fixing it. Money is too tight for repair jobs or new lawnmowers. She wonders if she could turn her tinkering skills into a paycheck which would support her family.

BLUE COLLAR WOMAN®

YES WE CAN

Dorothy Miller

Publisher
D. M. Morrisey
Atlanta, Ga 30328

D M Morrisey
Atlanta, Ga 30328

Copyright © 2011 by Dorothy Miller.
ISBN 978-0-9794146-2-6

All rights reserved.
This book may not be reproduced, in whole or in part, in any form, except in the case of brief quotations embodied in critical articles or reviews.

Printed in United States of America

Blue Collar Woman® is a trademark of Dorothy Miller
For more information, check the author's website at www.BLUECOLLARWOMAN.com or contact Dorothy Miller at dmiller@bluecollarwoman.com.

10 9 8 7 6 5 4 3 2 1

For Dr. Vanessa Roeder.
Thanks for lending me your Blue Collar dreams.

Vanessa Roeder is a surgeon in Tucson, Arizona. She shared her blue collar dreams with me while saving my life during a long battle with breast cancer. Perhaps some day we will renovate a house or build a shopping mall together.

Thank you to all those people in the Blue Collar skilled trades who gave me their time and opinions. Thank you also to the people responsible for the books and websites which were invaluable in the writing of this book. This includes especially the people at www.personalitypathways.com and www.personalitypage.com. Great accolades and thanks also to Chicago Women in Trades, Non Traditional Employment for Women (NEW), and Buckingham and Clifton, the authors of <u>Now, Discover your Strengths</u>. Visit their websites and let them know of your interest.

CONTENTS

1. Introduction 9

    You and Blue Collar Career
    Blue Collar: Careers, Jobs & Labels
    Are we there yet?

2. Skilled Trades: Your New Career...................... 39

    Why Choose a Blue Collar Skilled Trade
    Skilled Trades Opportunities

3. Passion, Power, Action............................ 67

    Yes You Can!
    Nine Steps to Job Satisfaction &
    Financial Freedom

4. Assess.. 87

    Assess your Self
    Assess Your Life
    Assess Your Job
    Assess Career Opportunities

5. Decide & Plan................................. 163

    Make Decisions for a New Life
    Plan, Review, Consult

6. Do It ... Live It.............................. 185

    Make it Happen: Schools, Training & Transition
    Make it Happen: Get a Job
    Live your New Life

Appendices..................................... 221

    Support Organizations for Women
    Research Tips
    Personality Types and Careers
    Apprenticeships & Technical Schools
    Career Info Example: Carpenters

BLUE COLLAR WOMAN®

Yes We Can!

1. INTRODUCTION

You and Blue Collar Careers

Are we there yet?

Why choose a Blue Collar Skilled Trade

You And Blue Collar Careers

This book is about reaching out for your own brand of HAPPINESS.

Are you happy? Successful? Are you financially secure? Do you love your job and your life? Are you passionate about your work? Do you love your job with a passion? OR ...

Love Your Job?

Hate Your Job?

Do you hate your job with a passion? If you know ... and, on most days, you are absolutely certain ... that you cannot stand your job for another day, then you need to consider a career change.

Also...money, money, money. If you just do not make enough money to live your life in a practical, desirable way, then look up, look around and step outside your box. How can you transform yourself and your life? .

You need to consider a career change if your gut says 'no more'. Your work is where you spend the greatest proportion of your time. Enjoying that work is a critical part of your happiness and your joy in life. So, consider this if your job is not right for you...

Is it time for a change?

This book is about reviewing basics and making decisions about your career, yourself and your life. It is about planning for and making the necessary life changes. It is about setting goals for yourself and growing into and achieving the goals you set.

Women have frequently not been made aware of the benefits and sheer personal satisfaction which can be derived from a career in one of the Blue Collar skilled trades. In this book, information about those trades and careers is highlighted.

Blue Collar Woman: Yes We can! offers a systematic approach, along with the information you need, to

> assess your SELF;
> assess your current work and life;
> define your goals;
> define your route to success; and
> to achieve those goals.

Considering a Blue Collar skilled trade as a career

There are a number of practical reasons to explore the Blue Collar skilled trades when you search for a good job and satisfying future. One of these careers can offer you the satisfaction of doing work that you like, work that is most suitable for your talents, and a job which offers you better pay, benefits and more flexible working hours. Consider what you want and need right now. Consider that, in the current career market, even a college degree may not offer the job opportunities, pay rate and benefits which are possible for a qualified Blue Collar skilled trades worker.

If you are thinking about a job change, then take the time to work through the assessment steps in Unit IV. If your self assessment and life assessment convinces you that a career change is the path you should take, then you should certainly consider one of the Blue Collar skilled trades. (By the way, **non traditional jobs** for women, we are told by the federal govt are those jobs which are traditionally held by men.)

Take a look at the following chart. This is an example of the lifetime difference in earnings potential for a Blue Collar skilled trade (carpenter) vs a traditional 'women's work' career (nurses assistant)

TRADITONAL	BLUE COLLAR SKILLED TRADE
Nurses Assistant	Journey level Carpenter
$9.44 per hour	$34.32 per hour
$19,635 per year	$71,386 per year
$589,056 in 30 years	$2,141,568 in 30 years

Difference:
$2,141,568 - $589,056 = $1,552,512

From the website of the Chicago Women in Trades organization (These figures are more than 12 years old now -- but they have not changed significantly over those intervening years.)

Independent Women with Confidence

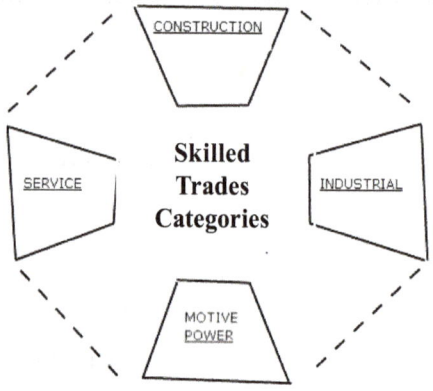

What are Blue Collar Skilled Trades jobs?

The Blue Collar skilled trades include a tremendous variety of skills and jobs - from plumber, carpenter and electrician to auto mechanic and air conditioning/heating technician and a lot of others which are not quite so well known. There are boiler repair technicians, air craft technicians, fleet installers, solar energy technicians, and people who lay out the dies and use the huge cutting machines in industry. There are fantastic jobs and large numbers of them. (*Take a look at Chapter 5, and the Blue Collar Woman® Wheel of Trades, to find out more about the job potential in the Blue Collar skilled trades career arena.*)

What do you need to know about getting into a Blue Collar skilled trade?

These jobs definitely require specialized skills. In fact, even when jobs are scarce, skilled trades jobs are almost always available and frequently go without applicants. The people who are out of work are not qualified for the skilled trades jobs which are available. These are jobs which require special education and training. The level of skill varies, of course, with the job. Getting an entry level job most often takes post high school technical classroom work and hands-on skills training. So, you need to know that it will take some effort to get the basics which you will need to get started. It can be done! It will, however, take determination, planning and hard work to make it happen.

There are several different paths which can lead you to your new career. Most involve formal or informal apprenticeships. The best of these is to be accepted into a formal apprenticeship program in your chosen career. This could be either through a union program and sponsorship or through one of the independent or company sponsored programs. These apprenticeships will pay you as you learn and get experience. Once you complete your formal education and training, you will graduate as a recognized, qualified technician in your chosen field. Alternatively, an informal apprenticeship would include attending a community college or technical school and getting a hands-on, entry level job through the local college - business community network.

How long will a career change take?

It can take 1 1/2 to 5 years to get to a level which qualifies you as skilled at a medium to expert level in your new career. However, you can be earning a good wage for your work well before that. In an apprenticeship program, you should be earning a pay rate based on a percentage of that for a journey level specialist. That pay rate should rise with your increasing expertise during the time you are getting your education and hands-on skills. Other training routes may not be so well defined as a formal apprenticeship program. In any case, you can expect to be earning a reasonable wage within eighteen months to two years and perhaps sooner. Obviously, you need to be prepared to sustain yourself and your family for some period of time during the transition.

Planning for that transition is a critical part of the process.

Is a skilled trades job for you?

What do you want from your job and your life? This book is about:

> Finding out about YOU -- your life, your d'ruthers, your goals. It is about learning more about BLUE COLLAR skilled trades. ... and it is about ... exploring what you need to know to make some life changing and career changing decisions? How do you make those decisions, build a plan and make the transition into a new life?

'Receptionist to Electrician,' Mary Lyndon told me, in a telephone interview from her new job in Illinois. At 36, she's making $22 an hour (plus benefits), in an entry level position, while learning to be an electrician. She's got two kids, a husband who (thankfully) thinks "our marriage is a partnership", and she has just completed a construction training class. She has zero, ('really zero-minus' she corrected) time in her busy schedule .... but she is making this career change work for her. Actually, Mary said, "I had only played with the idea of changing jobs ... my job was OK. Talk about the world crashing in and bringing disaster and magic in one 'fell swoop'", she said. "One day the company I worked for was there and the next, -**poof-,** we were all out the door." With no more similar jobs on any horizon, Mary decided to take the gamble and make a big change. With her options so limited, she thought it must be the right time to make the major move into something she had wanted for some time. This woman had dreamed of being an electrician. She thought I might think that strange, so she quickly rushed on to her explanation. Her dad was an electrician. She knew what the job meant... had played electrician as a child, even rebuilding her doll house with wires from her dad's job sites. Mary stopped to explain that she had taken a roll of wire which he needed for a project the next day. 'Boy, was he mad!' she remembered. 'Then he started laughing at her doll house rewiring job.'

So because she lost the OK job, Mary found the courage, time and determination to make this difficult change in the lives of herself and her family. With lots of help from family and friends, she made her plans and tackled the career and life change. Mary has just finished some 'in class' training and is on to more 'on the job' training.

You can hear the joy and excitement in her voice. 'Can you believe it,' she said. 'I just helped tear down a building and rebuild it'. Mary is thrilled with her new job. She has changed her life and thinks that her job doesn't seem like work-work anymore. She has definitely made a great start on a better future for her family.

So ...

Is a skilled trades job for you?

> What do you want from your job
> and
> your life?

BLUE COLLAR CAREERS, JOBS & LABELS

What does Blue Collar mean?

Blue Collar Worker, to most of us, means someone who works with their hands for a living. We probably think of 'that guy who comes in to fix the plumbing or works at the local auto shop' when we think blue collar. So, what is a blue collar skilled trades worker? Blue collar workers typically perform manual labor and earn an hourly wage. They usually do not have a college degree, although they are more and more likely to have post-high school education and training in their field. Many start as apprentices, learning their trade through classroom and hands-on work. Unions have traditionally played a major role in many of the blue collar jobs.

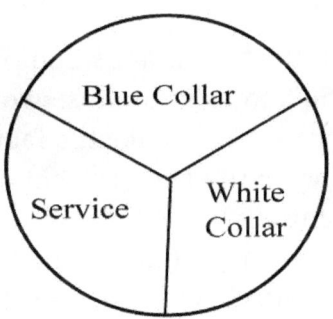

Most people distinguish blue collar workers by contrasting them with white collar and service workers. (Sounds right.) Really, though, the categories are not so cleanly separated, i.e. which jobs fit exactly into each category. However, the classifications do help to describe the types of jobs in the American scene. White collar jobs are generally office related. Of course, the term comes from the typical white shirt and suit of these office workers. Service jobs describe those where the workers interface with and/or assist others; for example, teachers, health care workers, and similar *people-to-people* jobs. Mostly, the white collar and service jobs are not considered manual labor.

Why the 'Blue Collar' name?

> *I remember my aunt and all her friends wore blue uniforms to work (in a garment factory) when I stayed with her one summer in the mountains of western North Carolina. My uncle was working in what he called 'the mica plant' and his uniforms were always heavy, dark blue and mostly smudged and dirty every evening. Had to be early fifties or before, I think.*

The term 'Blue Collar' first appeared, it seems, during the 1940's and '50's to refer to those workers doing primarily manual jobs in places like the factories in Detroit and Pittsburgh, the textile and garment industries in Appalachia and essentially the whole of the manufacturing explosion which occurred during and after World War II. These 'blue collar' workers typically wore heavy duty uniforms or protective clothing which were frequently blue -- and most definitely were NOT the white collar shirts and suits of the offices.

Unions, Blue Collar and American Middle Class

Each of us probably knows someone or has been personally directly impacted by the financial success of the unionization of the blue collar trades. A friend of my father worked in Pittsburgh as a blue collar worker during those decades of the power unions. He has retired now with a good pension and is proud to have been a part of it.

The early period of the 'blue collar workers' was a time when America was growing and producing and becoming. These blue collar workers became a large component in the expanding middle class of America. The workers were unionized and those unions helped to force better pay and working conditions for their members. The unions and the American Blue Collar workers together helped to create the American middle class. That middle class has essentially forged the culture, the economy and a unique way of life for America.

Blue Collar, Social Class and Education

Blue Collar and the Blue Collar worker, in our current American culture, unfortunately, hints of a lower social class. [Yes, America still has a class system -- but how those classes are defined is open to question and circumstance.] But this picture of a lower class Blue Collar worker is changing. An evolution is occuring in American culture. This is an evolution pushed by such forces as the economy, the political scene, and the increasing complexity of and skill requirements for Blue

Collar skilled trades. People can see that the skilled trades jobs are becoming more desireable. These careers demand better educated, highly trained workers and there is a growing recognition of the changing role of these skilled trades in American society.

The changing view of the Blue Collar skilled trades workers may, in fact, help to redirect the education system and public school goals. As a member of a trades council which was trying to advise a local school system, I found, along with the rest of the council members, that the school leaders were intent on directing students almost exclusively toward a college education. School counselors and administrators were firm in their opposition to any alternative suggestions.

However, this now appears to be changing ... ...with some really interesting notes.

The costs of a college education keep rising.

The financial status of many Americans is decreasing; and right now, in 2011, the middle class is being squeezed to near extinction.

Young people come out of the colleges frequently with hundreds of thousands of dollars of debt ... without a job and without the credentials or training necessary for a job in today's economy. We can all agree that there is a major place for a college education. Perhaps preparing for a career and an immediate job should be higher on the list of college goals in today's economy.

Although I do not have the answers, there must be someway that public school educators could provide a better jobs foundation, i.e. perhaps offering more alternatives for study and a more balanced (practical?) view of the career world to be faced.

Technical schools and community colleges are providing a different perspective and some excellent alternative education opportunities for those students who seek them out.

Blue Collar Today

Blue Collar manual labor is becoming increasingly more computerized and, increasingly, more highly skilled workers are needed. Blue Collar jobs are still with us. In many arenas, there are growing demands and plenty of jobs. However, many of those jobs are for people with different skills, a wider variety of skills and more education and training in their fields. The post high school technical schools and *community* schools are filling in the training and education gaps which are so important here.

Auto mechanics, electricians, assembly line workers ... have all seen the changes in their hands-on jobs. There are still Blue Collar jobs which require little skill or training; but fewer and fewer of these jobs exist. Many are being replaced, the jobs phased out or outsourced and those workers are being displaced. Also, the power of the unions is not as large a force in the marketplace and, thus, less a factor in the life of a typical Blue Collar worker. Those unions played a major role in obtaining rights and earnings for workers and the unions are still playing a large part in our society. However, there has been a shifting of the political and economic realities. Whatever the reasons, the number of union workers and their role in politics and the job markets is shrinking. How those changes will impact our society is still an open question. There are also continuing technology changes, outsourcing of jobs, increasing education costs, and a decreasing population of the American middle class. In addition, American manufacturing centers, like Detroit, have shut down and/or moved most of their operations to other world wide locations. These changes have produced panic level problems. We can argue and fight against some of the politics and economic trends. That's what a democracy is all about. However, the facts are that we must live in the real world, as it is. The changes, thankfully, have also created some great opportunities for those who have studied the situation and are ready to take advantage of it.

Some major factors which are playing the greatest roles in successful jobs and careers are the market place and 'supply and demand' of available workers and job requirements. That is especially true for these Blue Collar jobs. Money and opportunities are especially available now in some of the Blue Collar 'skilled' trades sectors. In addition, the cultural bias (where people have thought of Blue Collar workers as sitting on a lower rung of our informal class system) may also be changing.

My cousin was a lawyer and she used to grumble about the hourly charges of her electricians and plumbers when she had the typical home maintenance problems. I lost touch with her for a few years and when we finally reconnected, I was shocked a little, and also rather delighted that her new life had taken a huge ironic twist.

She is now an electrician. Said she always loved fixing things and has been fascinated by all things electric. So now she has a great business of her own and is a well known electrical subcontractor. ... ... No more grousing about electricians' bills.

ARE WE THERE YET?

"Are we there yet?"

Remember that old question when you were a kid driving to grandma's house for the holidays?

Well, we are definitely NOT there yet, girlfriend!

When it comes to working in the skilled trades, women make up less than 3% of skilled trades workers. In rough translation, that means less than three out of every one hundred of those highly paid crafts workers are women.

Don't get me wrong. Women are working as plumbers, electricians, welders, and in many other skilled trades jobs. I interviewed a house painter who has her own business, works alone, and usually makes over $70,000 a year. She loves it! And, she just rebounded into the work after a few years of an unsatisfactory post college job.

Congratulations and more power to you who have made it and are comfortable in your arena. Most of you are making a reasonable or even a great income and, hopefully, enjoying acceptance in these typical male enclaves. Or maybe you are working in your own little corner with your husband or partner in front of you? That's OK, too. In fact, good for you. You are THERE! Make it work for you.

Some unbelievable strides have been made since Rosie the Riveter got us started in the 1940's (Unfortunately, the Rosie's then mostly moved ... or were pushed?... back home when the men came back from war. But it was a good start.)

In 1964, women gained legal access to highly paid "non-traditional" jobs through passage of the Civil Rights Act which nominally renders discrimination against employees illegal on the basis of race, color, religion and sex. In 1978, the Department of Labor set affirmative action goals for hiring women on publicly financed construction sites. That sounded great! However, today, over thirty years later, women still make up less than 3 percent of skilled trades workers. This skilled trades arena has a workforce which has at any selected time between 4 and 6 million workers.

What a shock to find in my early research that there are so few women in Blue Collar trades. Even now, there's only a small proportion of women in the Blue Collar skilled trades. This is especially true in those areas where formal apprenticeships are required along with union membership. In researching the apprenticeship programs across the country, I found that several states are applying some special focus on bringing women into the Union Apprenticeship programs. However, there is still too little emphasis placed on attracting women into skilled Blue Collar trades. In one office, the people I talked with were great AND they could name all six women who were in the union apprentice program and currently in their training programs. They also were happy to tell me exactly where these women were and why they were chosen. However, people really do want to help and those support groups which are active are doing a fantastic job. However, I have to admit that I was surprised and distressed to hear that women are still not hearing about the opportunities and are still not getting through doors which were supposedly opened long ago.

What's the problem?

Women are not getting the word. It appears that the public schools have not been highlighting alternative career opportunities, like the skilled trades. They do not seem to be letting students know about these great career opportunities. In particular, many have not marketed, nor even made it sound suitable, for girls to seek out and show interest in these fields. Instead, for a long time, schools, including teachers, school counselors and administrators, have concentrated on pushing students toward college. Fifty years ago, it was OK for both Tom and Beth to go to a local trades high school (although Beth usually entered 'beauty culture' while Tom chose carpentry or plumbing). If you didn't think college was for you, there were alternatives. Guidance counselors talked with you about those opportunities; and schools made the training available. Young people could graduate with both a general education and the technical skills to get a good job. That's not so true anymore. I have talked with a number of those teachers who are involved in the remnants of 'shop classes'. Some have been integrated into the standard high school programs. However, the money for these programs seems to be scarce. It did seem for awhile that there would be a redirection back to some focus on these trades programs. Maybe?

Attitudes, harassment and closed doors.

The women who want into the skilled trades workforce often find that it is difficult to get in the door. The 'old boy' networks seem to be still strong, especially in the trade unions, including the apprenticeship programs. Once there, these women may face harassment, sometimes to an intolerable level. This can be in the form of small jokes at their expense, to broad slurs and actual touching and sexual innuendo.

Doesn't sound very inviting, does it?

Is it really worth it?

Yes!!! Absolutely.

...... Is it worth the *crap* you have to climb over to get in the door? Yes!

...... Is it worth the daily harassment, the mild 'jokes' or even the sexual slurs? Yes!

> First of all, that is going to die out, either from force of law and oversight by management or just the fact that so many women are going to push their way into the boy's playground. Second, and these reasons are best of all: the money, the benefits, the financial independence and security are there waiting for you. And, if your inherent strengths and talents lie in one of the skilled trades, learning those skills and doing the work each day --- that is ABSOLUTELY going to be a major factor in your lifelong happiness.

You have the right (or maybe you need to take those rights) to do the work that you want to do each day.

Help?

There are a growing number of organizations who want to help. Ask some of the sponsors and women in the Chicago Women in Trades program. Take a look at their website (www.cwit.org) and see what they are trying to do. They say it much better than I do:

> The herstory of the tradeswomen movement has been the struggle to survive as pioneers

in an unwelcoming world and to change conditions that prevent women from being fully integrated into well-paid blue-collar jobs. Despite gains in many professional occupations, women have yet to make significant inroads into skilled blue-collar careers.

Occupations in the trades are the key to many women's exit from welfare to a life of economic self-sufficiency for themselves and their families. Unlike careers typically dominated by women, for example child care and retail sales, characteristics of careers in the trades are wages up to $30 per hour, on-the-job training, pensions, and health care benefits through union membership. (See chart, "Lifetime Difference in Earnings.")

Unfortunately, many women and girls are continually locked out of these family-sustaining careers. For example, although 30% of the job opportunities in Illinois are in construction and manufacturing, women constitute only 3% of the construction workforce, and only 2.1% of the high-skill, high-wage manufacturing jobs. [Data from: The Illinois Department of Employment Security (IDES) Monthly statistical Summary, November 1999]. With 45% of households supported by women living below the poverty level and limitations imposed on welfare benefits, opening access to these family sustaining, career path occupations is critical both to assisting individual women achieve economic self-sufficiency and to changing perceptions of women's ability to perform these jobs.

Chicago Women in Trades direct service and advocacy programs for women and girls are dedicated to changing these statistics.

Here's a repeat of that chart from the website of the Chicago Women in Trades organization

---

TRADITIONAL   NONTRADITIONAL
Nurses Assistant   Journey level Carpenter
$9.44 per hour $34.32 per hour
$19,635 per year $71,386 per year
$589,056 in 30 years $2,141,568 in 30 years

Difference:
$2,141,568 - $589,056 = $1,552,512

This great organization, Chicago Women in Trades, and others like it, are all about how women can get started in the trades and achieve economic self-sufficiency.

> Skilled Blue Collar Trades jobs are a rich source of challenge, job satisfaction and financial security. There are more and more support groups, training opportunities, apprenticeships and jobs waiting for the woman who is ready to make it happen.

So...o...o

Why are we letting the men have all the FUN?...

the MONEY,

the OPPORTUNITY,

and the CHALLENGE?

YES

We have a ways to go ---

and

YES

We can make it happen,

One SUCCESS story at a time!!!

Why not make the next one
Your Success Story

Independent Women with Confidence

BLUE COLLAR WOMAN® Yes We Can!

2. Skilled Trades: Your New Career

Why Choose a Blue Collar Skilled Trade Career

Blue Collar: Skilled Trades Opportunities

Why Choose Blue Collar Skilled Trades?

Careers in the trades can offer fantastic opportunities ... good income, great benefits and jobs which may be exactly suited to your strengths, your talents and your d'ruthers. One of the skilled trades jobs may be just what you need to make you happy and successful.

The shortage of skilled workers in many of the blue collar trades is getting worse and this means that workers with those skills will be in high demand. The forecast is for more than a million job openings in this arena over the next 5-8 years. Many openings are the result of retirement by current workers. But many will be the result of new infrastructures, new projects, and new technologies. Economic downturns definitely will temporarily impact the demand for many of these jobs. However, the trend is for more blue collar skilled job opportunities -- world wide. That's real.

An estimated 15% or so of American workers (maybe about 25 million right now) are classified as blue collar by the US Bureau of Labor Statistics. The jobs range from minimum wage non skilled to highly skilled trades with people making over $100,000 a year. Choosing to join this newly emerging workforce of highly skilled trades workers makes a lot of sense.

In America, yes ... there has been some cultural stigma associated with blue collar jobs. However, that is changing with the changing job scenarios. And, anyway, what about that? ONE: do you care? If you are in a job you love and making great money and you and your family are happy and better off, how much do you care? Will it make a difference in your life? and TWO: this attitude is changing. There are pent up forces at work here, like the growing recognition of the importance of these skilled jobs and the growing scarcity of the people to do the work. College degrees are expensive and no longer a guarantee of a good job. The Blue Collar skilled trades include great jobs, with good pay, and life satisfaction. The emphasis on college in the public schools as the only acceptable route may be finally changing. Even though women frequently are being actively steered away from them, those women need to research the jobs and the job markets carefully. Blue Collar skilled trades jobs are some of the best opportunities available ... for *anyone* looking for a good career.

Not only is a skilled trade career a good choice for the individual, it is good for society. (Not really our first concern -- but still interesting and good to know.) The growing number of jobs and the decreasing numbers of qualified workers means that our economy, our infrastructures, our industries desperately need you.

There is also the opportunity to more easily become your own boss. Many of the skilled trades workers in the construction business are contractors and subcontractors. They own their own businesses and make their own success in the trades. Most of the entrepreneurs I talked with love this aspect of the job. They like being their own boss, working their own hours and creating success for themselves.

The skilled trades worker sees and experiences the end result of the work - *the final product.* For those who love such hands-on creativity, this is a gift without price.

The relative ease of entry into the skilled trades is another reason for taking on one of these jobs. You can jump into a skilled trades job through training and an apprenticeship where you can learn and earn a living at the same time.

So --

> A Blue Collar Skilled Trade is an excellent career choice.

Next, we'll talk more about WHY the choice can be a good choice for YOU.

So ... why choose a Blue Collar Skilled Trades career? Let's take a look at just a few of those reasons.

1. You *want* the job because you know you like the work.

Reason number one to choose a Skilled Trades Career is that you truly WANT it. Don't spend effort, time and money getting into a new career (whatever it is) until you know 'pretty much' for sure that you want it. How do you know if a skilled trades career is for you? You explore yourself: your skills, temperament, experiences, needs, d'ruthers and goals and compare those to the required skills and opportunities for Blue Collar skilled trades jobs. Pretty simple, right? Well ... ... You'd be surprised at the number of people who skip this step and jump right into the job change/job entrance process. Sure, you need to spend some careful time researching jobs, where the jobs are, what are the work environments, requirements, both physical and mental -- -- but - first, you need to spend the quality time with yourself -- to research, explore and understand YOU!

Keep reading! More about the GREAT jobs coming up. *And*, we will talk more about YOU and knowing yourself. Find out what you really want and whether you are suited for a Skilled Trades career.

2. Great Job Opportunities.

The skilled trades are incredibly diverse. There are over 140 apprenticeable trades, in four separate sectors: Construction, Industrial, Motive Power, and Service.

You will work with your hands, with your mind and in a wide variety of tasks. These are mostly jobs which are common wherever you live. Plumbers, electricians, tile setters, painters, and lots more. No need to travel to exotic places. (But you can, if you wish. There are lots of countries looking for skilled trades workers. Remember, we live in a global economy nowadays.) There are a lot of different types of jobs. We will explore some of them here and you can go online to our website, www.bluecollarwoman.com, and many other websites to find more. During the good times, there are lots of jobs available in your hometown. In the lean times, it makes sense that there will be better offerings for people with the most skilled trades experience.

3. Career Choices. Wide variety of basic skills.

You may not have the finger dexterity or training to play a piano. But you may have the hand - eye coordination needed to thread a pipe, along with the smarts to check out a wiring schematic. You can learn the techniques for professional painting, for tile setting, for running a machine lathe or building and installing a closet or cabinet. There are a lot of job choices -- and a wide variety of required skills. You will most likely find that one set of those skills will fit your 'needs, talents, d'ruthers, and capabilities.'

You may not be a study/book learning guru. That does not mean that you are not smart or that you are limited in your job choices. Take a look at the chapters on learning about yourself and your capabilities. The skilled trades offer an unbelievable array of careers based on your combination of strengths, desires and aptitudes.

4. Fast, relatively easy career entry.

It can take several years from the time you decide that you want to make a career change to becoming qualified in some of the skilled trades. You could well need up to five years to complete a formal apprenticeship and become fully certified in your selected field. However, you should be earning a fairly decent wage well before then. Alternatively, many plumbers and other local tradespeople take on trainees or helpers. As a 'helper', you may take on the role of trainee if you work with your boss in a positive manner. If you take the school-only route, it can seem like a long time before you are earning a good wage, depending on your circumstances. That is especially true if you are down to your last few dollars and aren't living with your parents. However, compared to alternative life and career choices, the time investment is relatively short. Let no one tell you it will be easy. However, time to earning a paycheck is shorter and the financial investment can be significantly lower than going for a college degree. (A note about college: Do not let the time and money investment deter you. IF YOU WANT TO GO TO COLLEGE - FIND A WAY TO MAKE IT HAPPEN. There is financial and other assistance out there. Do some research. You can find a way.)

For skilled trades careers, there are local community colleges and technical programs which are low cost. Tuition assistance is frequently available. This incudes formal or informal programs which are paid for by local businesses as part of a work to learn or apprenticeship program. There may be some high school and local school district programs in your area which offer training. Some school districts seem to be again exploring and offering some technical based alternatives to a four year, standard college program.

If you can cross the barriers to getting into them, union and independent apprenticeship programs are great. These are an excellent way to break into your selected trade. Women's groups, unions and independent building associations are also out there. Talk to them. Many are ready to help you jump in.

5. Good Money.
Sound financial future.

Skilled trades jobs offer excellent wages plus benefits. In many cases, these will match or exceed the salaries of college graduates. This is not only true of the starting salaries. The outlook for getting and keeping a job has proven much better and financially more stable for the skilled trades worker than a typical college graduate in many vocations. In addition, reviewing our discussion regarding the time, effort and money it takes to get into a skilled trades career, the comparison with a full college education cost/financial rewards is excellent. There are also some studies which indicate that there is a world wide crisis coming. The forecast is for many fewer skilled trades workers than we need. For the skilled trades worker, the future looks good.

6. Improving Workplace for Women

Things are gradually getting better for women in the workplace. There are continuing practical issues and challenges to be faced. And, yes, there is still a lot of discrimination and harassment out there... ... still lots of places where women are neither welcome nor even tolerated. However, there are also a lot of changing attitudes. It is possible for a woman to work in a previously 'male only' job, excel, and be accepted for the work accomplished. That is becoming more possible with each generation. If you want to do a job -- if you can excel in it and know you are good -- **GO FOR IT!**

> ***Don't look for obstacles, but be practical when you encounter them.***

Workplace harassment is, hopefully, slowly fading into a ghost of the past. (Well, nothing like looking at the positive side, right?) There is a lot to be said on this topic and we women need to be discussing it and working toward resolutions, both in specific personal instances and for all of us.

So ...

Why Choose a Skilled Trades Career?

> Reasons for choosing a Blue Collar Skilled Trades career are many and as varied as each individual who explores career options. What does your 'gut' tell you abour what you like, don't like, and what is possible for you? What do you want to do? and ... Can you get excited about your decision and making it happen for you?

BLUE COLLAR
Skilled Trades Opportunities

Blue Collar Skilled Trades:
Lots of different types of skills involved in each trade. Lots of different types of jobs, careers.

There are some excellent, newly emerging and evolving jobs which require specialized training and highly developed skills. These jobs pay extremely well and can be challenging and provide very satisfying careers. They offer a great alternative to college with a lot less up-front time and money investment. *And,* a great thing for a beginner is that you can get into a blue collar skilled trade -- into your own chosen field -- through apprenticeships. There are 200 or more separate jobs. In over 140 of those blue collar skilled trades, you can join and get your formal training and initial on-the-job work through apprenticeships.

An *apprenticeship* is a combination of on-the-job-training and classroom studies where you learn the practical and theoretical aspects of a blue collar skilled trade. An apprentice is supervised by a journey-level craftsperson. It takes several years to become fully trained, depending on the trade. (A journey-level worker is just what you would expect - someone who already has the skills and experience to do the job.)

For many apprenticeship programs, there are support groups which provide preliminary education and training which can help prepare you for acceptance into the program. The demand for these preparatory programs may be intense in your area; however, the rewards make them a very wise choice and worth the

effort. In one pre-apprenticeship program, offered by NEW (Non Traditional Employment for Women www.new-nyc.org) in New York City, the focus they say is on:
> *hands-on instruction in carpentry, electrical wiring, and plumbing; applied math; tool safety and identification; physical conditioning; and exploring nontraditional careers.*

For Your Information (FYI) and... guess what!... ... Blue Collar Skilled Trades are identified as 'nontraditional occupations' by the government. Like much of the information I found, I didn't know this when I started exploring. The U.S. Department of Labor has a definition for lots of things I never knew were formally defined by the government. One of these is for 'nontraditional occupations'. They define it as

"occupations ... ... in which women comprise less than 25 percent of the total workers."

So what does it matter how they are classified? Right? Well, it could make a difference in getting help in transitioning into one of these careers (or NOT).

And, also, guess what!

That **'non-traditional'** category -- that category includes a LOT of jobs. The NEW (Non traditional Employment for Women) group in New York City says that **they** focus on *"skilled blue-collar work, because it pays more and provides better benefits, even to those without college degrees."*

> *We include in this chapter only an overview of the potential job opportunities. See www.bluecollarwoman.com for more sources. There is a lot of job information available online. Use it to research and analyze your career choices.*

There are over 140 blue collar skilled trades which you can enter through apprenticeships in most areas of the US and Canada. Most of these skilled trades may be included in the categories of: Construction, Industrial, Service and Motive Power.

Much of the information related to these trades was found

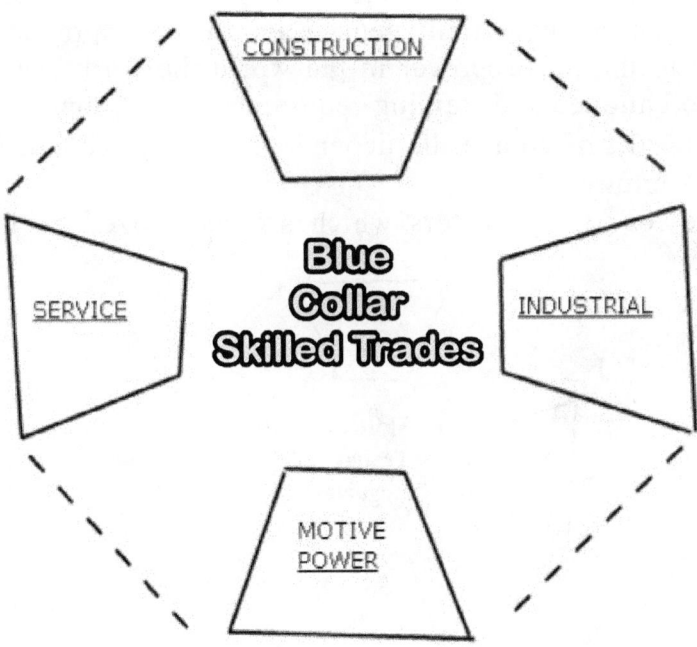

Independent Women with Confidence

in the websites for www.tradeability.ca. Tradeability.ca is an Employment Ontario Program funded in part by the Government of Canada. There are also a number of other great websites which give more information on the skilled trades.

Both the United States and the Canadian governments collect and provide extensive data on jobs, employment and careers.

In this chapter, I will also discuss these skilled trades and categories as they are described by US government sources.

In order to give you a preliminary picture of the richness and potential offered by a career in the blue collar skilled trades, I will describe these categories of careers, the jobs included and will give a few more details about a few of the specific jobs. The information is not specific to the United States or Canada, in most cases. The jobs are essentially generic and the descriptions apply to the job wherever in the world the work occurs. The entrance and training requirements and opportunities will, of course, be dependent on local economies and cultures.

The four trade sectors which are recognized by the

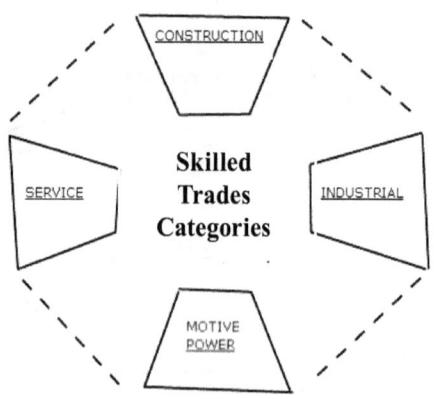

Canadian program *(tradeability.ca is an Employment Ontario Program funded in part by the Government of Canada)* are:

Construction. These are skilled trades involved in the building and/or installation services for homes, schools, office buildings and institutions. The specific topics covered in Building and Construction, include such structural areas as architecture, design, framing, and structural trades. There are jobs and businesses in this category which are particularly appealing from many points of view, i.e. economic, creative and personal satisfaction. For example, carpenters are skilled construction workers. (Other skilled construction occupations are listed in the next section.)

Industrial. This category of trades involves product manufacturing and equipment maintenance. Examples include tool and die maker, industrial millwright, mechanic, and cabinetmaker.

Motive Power. Trades in this sector relate to repair and service of automobiles, transportation equipment and small engines. Examples include automotive service technician, truck and bus technicians, as well as, heavy duty equipment techs and mechanics.

Service. This is a broad and diverse sector which includes those trades which provide some specific support (service) and frequently interface directly with others. These skilled trades include hairstylist, child care, classroom assistant and cook. (Some of these sound like service sector and also like more traditional 'women's jobs', right?)

So - let's next take a look at what some of these jobs are and then, we will review one of them in more detail.

Keep in mind that the object of this discussion is to familiarize you with the types of jobs and opportunities. Go to www.bluecollarwoman.com for more research and source information.

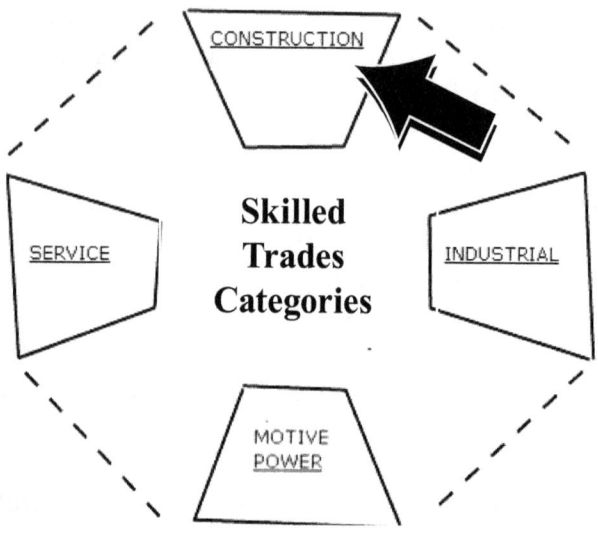

Construction - Skilled Trades Jobs
Trades involved in the build and/or install services for homes, schools, office buildings and institutions.

Most of the jobs and the classifications listed are found in the websites for www.tradeability.ca. Tradeability.ca is an Employment Ontario Program funded in part by the Government of Canada.

Brick and Stone Mason
Cement Finisher
Cement Mason
Construction Boiler Maker
Construction Craft Worker
Construction Millwright
Drywall, Acoustic And Lathing Applicator
Drywall, Finisher And Plasterer
Electrician, Construction and Maintenance
Electrician, Domestic and Rural
General Carpenter
Glazier and Metal Mechanic
Heavy Equipment Operator/Dozer Operator
Heavy Equipment Operator/Tractor Loader, Backhoe Operator
Heavy Equipment Operator/Excavator Operator
Hoisting Engineer: Mobile Crane Operator, Br. 1
Hoisting Engineer: Mobile Crane Operator, Br. 2
Hoisting Engineer: Tower Crane Operator
Ironworker
Painter and Decorator, Commercial And Residential
Painter and Decorator, Industrial
Plumber
Powerline Technician
Refrigeration/Air Conditioning Systems Mechanic
Roofer
Sheet Metal Worker
Sprinkler and Fire Protec
Steamfitter

Exterior Insulated Finishing Systems Mechanic
Floor Covering Installer
Hazardous Materials Worker
Heat And Frost Insulator
Native Residential Construction Worker
Precast Concrete Erector
Precast Concrete Finisher
Reinforcing Rod Worker
Residential Air Conditioning Systems Mechanic
Restoration Mason
Terrazzo, Tile And Marble Setter

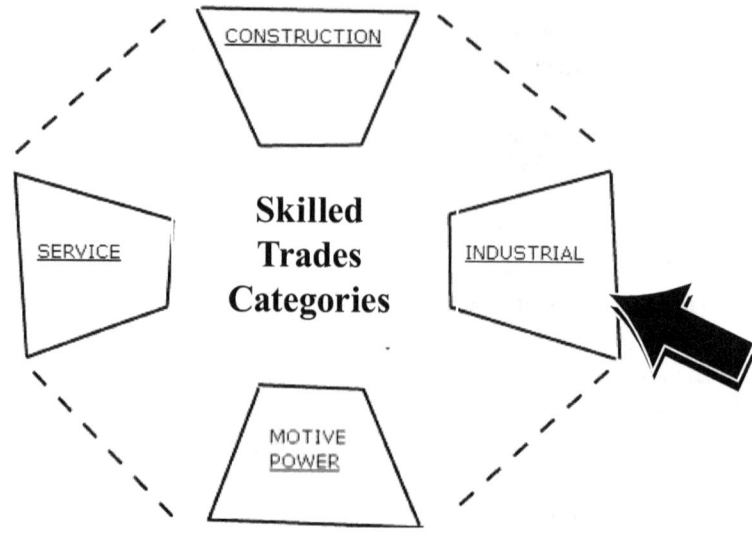

Industrial - Skilled Trades Jobs

Trades involving product manufacturing and equipment maintenance.

Aircraft Maintenance Engineer
Cabinetmaker
Elevating Devices Mechanic
Entertainment Industry Power Technician
Facilities Maintenance Mechanic
Facilities Systems Technician
General Machinist
Industrial Electrician
Industrial Mechanic Millwright
Machine-Tool Builder and Integrator
Mould Maker
Pattern Maker
Precision Metal Fabricator
Tool and Die Maker
Tooling/Tool Maker
Welder

Bearings Mechanic
Blacksmith
CNC Programmer
Composites Structures Technician
Die Designer
Draftsperson, Mechanical
Draftsperson, Plastic Mould Design
Draftsperson, Tooling And Die Design
Electrical Control (Machine) Builder
Electrical Motor System Technician
Electrician - Power House Operator (TTC)
Electrician - Signal Maintenance (TTC)
Fitter (Structural Steel/Plate Worker, Steel Fabricator)
Fitter Welder
Fitter-Assembler (Motor Assembly - Large Motors)
Hydraulics/Pneumatics Mechanic
Industrial Instrument Mechanic
Locksmith
Mould Designer
Mould Or Die Finisher
Optics Technician (Lens And Prism Maker)
Packaging Machine Mechanic
Process Operator: Refinery, Chemical And Liquid Process
Pump Systems Installer/Mechanic
Railway Car Technician
Relay and Instrumentation Technician*
Roll Grinder/Turner
Saw Filer/Fitter
Ski Lift Mechanic
Surface Blaster
Surface Mount Assembler
Thin Film Optician
Tool And Cutter Grinder
Tool And Gauge Inspector
Water Well Driller

Independent Women with Confidence

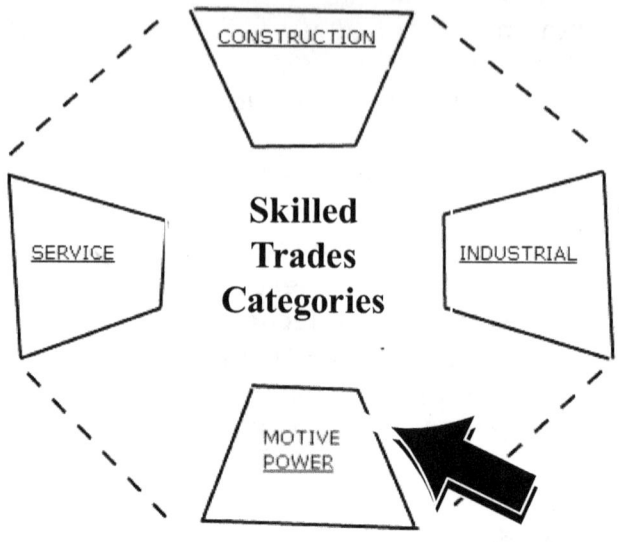

Motive Power - Skilled Trades Jobs

These are jobs like auto mechanic, i.e. anything which has to do with machines that move.

Agriculture Equipment Technician
Auto Body and Collision Damage Repairer
Auto Body Repairer
Automotive Glass Technician
Automotive Painter
Automotive Service Technician
Heavy Duty Equipment Technician
Marine Engine Mechanic
Motive Power Machinist
Motorcycle Technician
Parts Technician
Powered Lift Truck Technician
Recreation Vehicle Technician
Small Engine Technician
Turf Equipment Technician
Truck and Coach Technician
Truck and Trailer Service Technician

Alignment And Brakes Technician
Automotive Electronic Accessory Technician
Fuel And Electrical Systems Technician
Tire Wheel And Rim Mechanic
Transmission Technician

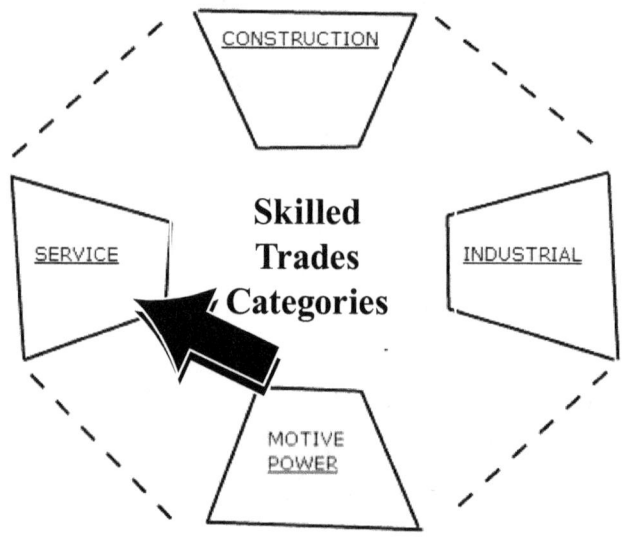

Services - Skilled Trades Jobs

Trades which provide some specific support (service) and frequently interface directly with others. (Blue Collar job categories may or may not include some of these jobs - depending on the source and the context. For our purposes, if your are interested - go for it. Doesn't matter the label.)

Agriculture Dairy Herdsperson
Agriculture Swine Herdsperson
Agriculture Fruit Growe
Arborist/Landscaper
Baker
Baker-Patissier
Chef
Child and Youth Worker
Cook - Assistant, Branch 1
Cook, Branch 2.
Developmental Services Worker
Early Childhood Educator
Educational Assistant
Electronic Service Technician.
Hairstylist
Hardware, Lumber and Building Materials Retailer
Horticultural Technician
Information Technology
Contact Centre - Customer Care Agent
Information Technology
Contact Centre - Inside Sales Agent
Information Technology
Contact Centre - Technical Support Agent
Information Technology Hardware Technician
Information Technology Network Technician
Network Cabling Specialist

more about
Skilled Trades Jobs

For each of these skilled trades jobs listed, there is excellent information gathered and published by government and many other sources. Check out the US Department of Labor, as well as, the Canadian government's similar website. Lots more information there. Most of the support groups listed in the Appendix A also have information and website links which will help. This information can help you to decide what your career choice should be.

Of course, you will be familiar with many of the jobs because we all come into contact with these workers in everyday living. However, in order to make a career choice, you need a deeper understanding of Blue Collar Skilled Trades job opportunities and the requirements.

Research these jobs. Find one or more which suits you, your family and you needs, d'ruthers, and lifestyle. There are some excellent opportunities.

> *The top level information wheel for CARPENTERS is included in Appendix E. Take a look. See what you think.*

BLUE COLLAR WOMAN® Yes We Can!

3. Passion, Power, Action

**YES
YOU
CAN**

**Nine Steps to
Job Satisfaction and
Financial Freedom**

YES YOU CAN!

> Positive Thinking... ... ...
> Self Generating Power ... ...
> Passion... ...
> Self Knowledge... ...
> Action Planning ... ...
> START NOW... ...

Those are key words and key thoughts on which to base a life of passion and happiness. You CAN make a career change and that change can transform your life. You can do this if you know what you want, seek it with passion and generate your own power to make it happen. This means that you define your own special goals and map the route to get you to those goals, i.e. that route includes the process and steps involved in the transition to your new career. You also need to understand and clearly define for yourself why the results are so important to you. In fact, a career change may be the single most significant (also, the most difficult) transformation in your life. It can make the difference in your level of personal happiness for the rest of your life. The right job will bring focus and a daily passion for living. You can love going to work and look forward to it with pleasure.

What do you spend your time doing on a daily basis? Your job takes a lot of that time. You need to choose your new career carefully. You can make a dramatic difference in your life with the right new career.

Happiness is ...

Learn what makes you happy in your work. Then find a way to do it. Happiness is ... doing what you love to do. You can make this new career happen if you understand what you want and are convinced that a new life is waiting. You must also be convinced that the new life will be focused and filled with passion, with happiness and with challenge and hope. The right career can provide the focus. Your strengths, personality and drive will provide the rest.

A job that you like is the most central and tangible ingredient in personal happiness. Happiness has been defined in many ways. When you are totally focused, in the moment, on some activity which you love doing and which you do well ... that's a pure form of happiness. You may not recognize it as happiness at the time, but, if you can re-enact that moment, you will see your own happiness. During that time, you are living completely in the moment and the activity. The best jobs give us that kind of happiness. That is a key ingredient in living a happy life.

Joy in life, or what we loosely term *happiness* has, I think, five primary 'passion' foundations --

> Something to do that you love;
> Someone to be with whom you love;
> Something to look forward to with hope;
> Finances sufficient to your needs; and
> Health and physical well being.

Personality and Success

<u>Power Generator.</u> You can make that new life happen if you can change the mode on your internal power generator from *I think I can* -- to -- *I will do this*. Once that mindset has been created, once you fully believe that this is a fact which now just needs to become reality --- then you will achieve that reality. That's some of the message from the last five books I read on positive thinking and accomplishment. A lot has been written on the subject. However, what those books usually boil down to is essentially this rule --

You can do it if you know you **will** do it.

OK -- Yes, I believe it! And, still, it sounds a little *hokey* even to me. But... this I do know. It works! Once you change the terms in your mind from "I'll try" to "I'll do", then a major hurdle has been crossed. Then you can envision your goal and a path for getting there. The doing may still be a major struggle -- but, at this point, your will has kicked in. It may then still be a *step by step* slugfest, but the steps will be taken. I am always utterly amazed at what the human spirit can accomplish.

My friend, Darlene, has three children, an ex-husband who has disappeared and a mother who has Alzheimer's. She has text books on the toilet, text books by her bed, and text books on the kitchen counters. Frequently the house is in disarray (actually, it is so awful sometimes that I visit just to clean house and listen to her litany of school, house, children and work woes. Makes me REALLY appreciate that the similar time for me is in the past.) It sometimes seems impossible to live the lives that many single women with small children exist in. If that is where you are, just know this, others have been there and made it through. There are people and groups out there who can help. (See the appendices for specific groups and how to find more of them in your area) There are jobs and training you can get. Some of these groups will provide support, such as child care and health benefits.

If you are in school and don't see a way to get to college, or even have any desire to attend college, you need to consider how to make yourself a path into something you will enjoy. A Blue Collar skilled trade may be for you!

If you are fifty two (or sixty two or whatever) years old and have been doing the same, dead-end job for the last thirty five of those years - do you want to change? Do you hate it (still) but think it is stupid to make a move at this later stage in your career? I say to you: *Ridiculous!* MAKE THE MOVE!

Now is Now *What if'ing* yourself and your life doesn't do anything but cause frustration and depression (unless, of course, you stop wallowing and turn those *what if's* into plans for current and future actions.) **Now** is the only place you can start to live a different life. Now is where you are.

Three P Mindset

Mary Swinson has been called 'little Mary' from age eight or so. Not really relevant here, just interesting. Anyway, Mary is an admirable person. She has started her own company, raised three children without a partner, and is now recovering from the loss of that company, which was almost like a fourth child to her. So, I expected to find her under the couch and trembling with tears and fears when I dropped by to see her the other day.

Wow, was I surprised! Mary was on the phone, extolling her plans for a new company to a potential investor. She was smiling, talking, beckoning me in with a couple of quick nods of her head, balancing a tray with a couple of glasses of iced tea and heading for the back door to deliver the tea to one of her sons, who had dropped by from his last class at the local community college to mow the lawn.

It is a cliche to say that everyone loves Mary. She is one of those people who walk into a room and everyone immediately turns to find the sudden light source. Short, blondish, fortiesh, and not a great beauty ... Mary has a charisma which is dynamic and she glows with an aura which reflects her love of life. This woman knows how to listen and each person is special to her and each one knows it. But the 'Mary' qualities we need to concentrate on here are especially critical in achieving and living a new career and defining a new life for yourself.

There is a **ThreeP mindset** which drives the true achievers of this world. These P traits are the mental driving force for success and they are not a secret formula. Every successful person I know reflects those traits. Each one is ***positive, proactive and passionate***. These words reflect that mindset and they resound with power. When you are near such a person, you hear and see and feel the power. If you can incorporate these character traits into your own personality, these three power P's, then you can achieve miracles, rule the world, or more important --- make for yourself a good life.

Positive Attitude

Who are those people who 'knock your socks off' when they walk into a room... ...who create a swirling circle of others who are drawn to their light, their delight in life. They also leave a trail of happier people, and almost as naturally to their mental structure, they create success and satisfaction for themselves and others as they go. Each of these power whirlwinds sees, absorbs and reflects automatically the positive side of any situation and each has a core which is focused, positive and shining with that positive attitude and outlook on life. With such an attitude, even the most difficult becomes easier.

Someone told me something once which I have observed over and over again:

> There are the life enriching, positive personalities, but, unfortunately, there are also those who are innate victims in this world.

Both these attitudes really have little to do with the people or events surrounding them. It is very much about the internal character of the person. The 'victims' are the people who always see themselves as defeated. This *victim* personality is always certain that others are against them. They are 'put upon' by the world and nothing seems to change that attitude.

Then there are others, those who are never defeated for long. The motto of these people is: Pick yourself up, dust yourself off and march off again. These winners also are sure that the world is for them *and* they are for the world. They see each new person in that world as a new adventure and a potential new friend. They see each new task as a success in their life; each new failure as an opportunity to learn;
    and, they try again.
    And again. *And again.*

Passion

Passion is so closely associated with sensual love and sex that it is sometimes difficult to understand the word in a more general context.

But that passion which can be felt and experienced during a sexual encounter is exactly the intensity and feeling that we need to bring to our daily living experience. That intensity, concentration, focus, and love is a reflection of how a life may be lived... ... with intensity and love of the moment and the life.

    Passion is the real power driver for living.

We live with passion, if we are intensely involved, focused and driven by our interest in and concentration on the moments of this life. ... We need to find the careers, the people, the drivers for our lives which create that intensity of feeling ... that passion.

But, how do you teach someone to live and experience life with passion? We can explain, define, describe.

But, others cannot create for you this feeling of intensity and focus and love of life which should guide the choices you make and live. You must choose the career, the life partner, the friends and avocations, the way you spend your time and mental energies which will create for you this passion. The opposite side of the coin is that, without passion, you will not live to your fullest. ***You will not experience the full joy of the moments of your days.***

Although this passion for life is perhaps an innate strength (maybe you are born with it), everyone must have some of those moments of focused joy in daily life.

> If you can recognize those moments and isolate them in your memory, then you can build on them. If each *passion* moment can be recognized, you can etch that feeling of joy into your psyche. Like any learning experience, you can use the recognition, the remembrance, and replay of those passion moments to strengthen and grow your capability to live a life with passion.

Without this passion, even with a great new career --- happiness will still be elusive. You will wonder why you made such an effort for so little reward. A new job can be great. However, if you cannot recognize and create, understand and live with a passion for life,
> then...
>> Stay where you are.
>>> Not much is going to change for you.

Proactive

Being proactive means that a person will seek out solutions, think outside the proverbial box, and take steps toward achievement. Decide what to do and do it. Action is that key word in our unit title: Passion, Power, Action. In many cases, it is so much easier to take what life brings to you. I have even heard this defined as a great philosophy of life:

> *God, some greater power, fate, or the Universe will send what you need. Wait for the chance, the opportunity will come, then you can take advantage and step into it. God provides what is needed.*

But, I think waiting for fate, or even your God, to intervene in your life is no way to live. **You** must decide what you want, how you want to live, and then make it happen for you and your family.

No one else is going to tell you what to do and when to do it.

Well, someone else may try to tell you what to do and when to do it. But, you should have graduated from all those you depended on to tell you what to do ...Your mom, your dad, your best teacher and even your school's permanent record department. You may listen to advice. But make your own decisions. You are your own motivator ... your own producer, director and reviewer. You will have to envision each step then make it happen. Critique the results for yourself.

If you fail, you'll surely know it. Get up. Figure out what you did wrong. Do it again. A lttle better this time, hopefully. That's life and that's great living and joy.

Clarify your Goals; Plan; Play to your Strengths; Envision Success

Personal Strengths

If you love doing something and you do it well, count that as one of your own personal strengths. If you do something well but you really don't like doing it, don't do it. That's both simple and difficult. Try not to get caught up in the expectations of others -- and be forced into doing something you don't like. When you choose a new job, a new career, think about your own strengths, likes and yearnings and use that knowledge of yourself. Choose based on your strengths and the potential for using those strengths in any new job. Your personal strengths are those things that you love to do and that you do well. Keep in mind that skills and knowledge can be learned. Love for the activity combined with innate basic abilities are strengths which are just there within you. Mostly, these are not very changeable. Go for your strengths and you will make a good choice. Choose a job which will make you want to go to work each day.

Goals

Clarify your goals. What do you want to achieve? What are the specific results? If you choose to be a plumber, then describe for yourself what that will mean. Will you work for someone else and change out faucets, dig up frozen water lines and fix clogged drains? What kind of plumber will you be? What will your financial goals and other expectations be? Don't surprise yourself at the end of the transition. Make sure that the road to a new life leads to the new life you want.

Plan

Sit down with a paper and pencil and make a list of the actions you must take to get to your final goal. Make sure you understand each step and have included each step.

Envision Success

The big achievers are those who engage in mental role playing. Learn how to do this. You can call it dreaming, meditating, or role playing. Envision the steps before you make them and continually envision success. What will that mean? See it in your mind: *doing the new job ... taking your kids to school ... and going on to work.* Feel the joy as you prepare for each new day at the new job. Keep those visions in your head and do whatever it takes to reach that goal.

Follow the Golden Rules

Rule 1: Start now!

Pick a thread and start pulling. Start where you are. Start with something which is doable for you NOW. It can be a small thing. But plan for that action to move you forward an inch or so toward a planned goal.

Rule 2: Iteration makes for achievement.

Life Layers and iteration. If you start somewhere in a process, you can go back through the process again. With each step, you will learn more: more about yourself, about the process, about the skill set. That iteration is an excellent learning tool. Don't feel that you have failed the first (or fifth) time through. Pick yourself up; do it again. We learn and we build our self, our self confidence and our lives in a series of *life layers*. An iteration result is not a failure.

Rule 3: Failure is essential to success.

An iteration result is not a failure ... **if** *...*
you pick yourself up, figure out what went wrong, and go on to the next try. You just learned a little more on the road to success.

Think about how a baby learns to walk. Have you watched? One day the tot is crawling along the floor. She drags herself up somehow and takes a few steps. Falls on her beautiful little butt, cries for a bit, then picks herself up again and takes a few more steps.

Rule 4: There are three primary aspects to achieving and living a new career and a new life ---

- your positive attitude, determination, and mindset,
- the new career you choose for yourself, and
- the lifestyle YOU plan and mold for yourself.

9 STEPS TO YOUR NEW LIFE

What do you have to do to change careers and start a new, better life? First, I think you must be sure that this is what you want. By the time you finish the assessment and decision process, you should have rethought your career choices and primary decisions and essentially become more sure that you want this change.

Why do you need to be so sure? You need to understand that this is not an easy path. Whether you are choosing a new career for the first time or the fifth time, the process can be difficult. There are a number of steps involved which are essential. You may decide to skip some of these. However, skipping steps means you take the chance of making decisions based on information you do not have. Those decisions may have a large impact on your life.

Be Sure. Check your premises, do your research, walk through each suggested step. If you are going to skip one, understand why you feel you can do so. Do you already have the information involved in that step of the process? Do you feel you already know the goal so well that you can skip 'to the chase'?

Remember that life is built up of layers of trials, slices of living and multiple iterations through plans and actions. The only real failure is the failure to get back up and try again.

Nine Steps

Lot's of Work

**A New Career!
A New Life!**

1. Assess Your SELF

2. Assess Your Job

3. Assess Your Life

4. Assess Career Opportunities

5. Make Decisions for a New Life

6. Plan, Review, Consult

7. Make it Happen: Training and Transition

8. Make it Happen: Get a Job

9. Live your New Life

BLUE COLLAR WOMAN®
Yes We Can!

4. ASSESS

Assess Yourself

Assess Your Life

Assess Your Job

Assess Your Career Opportunities

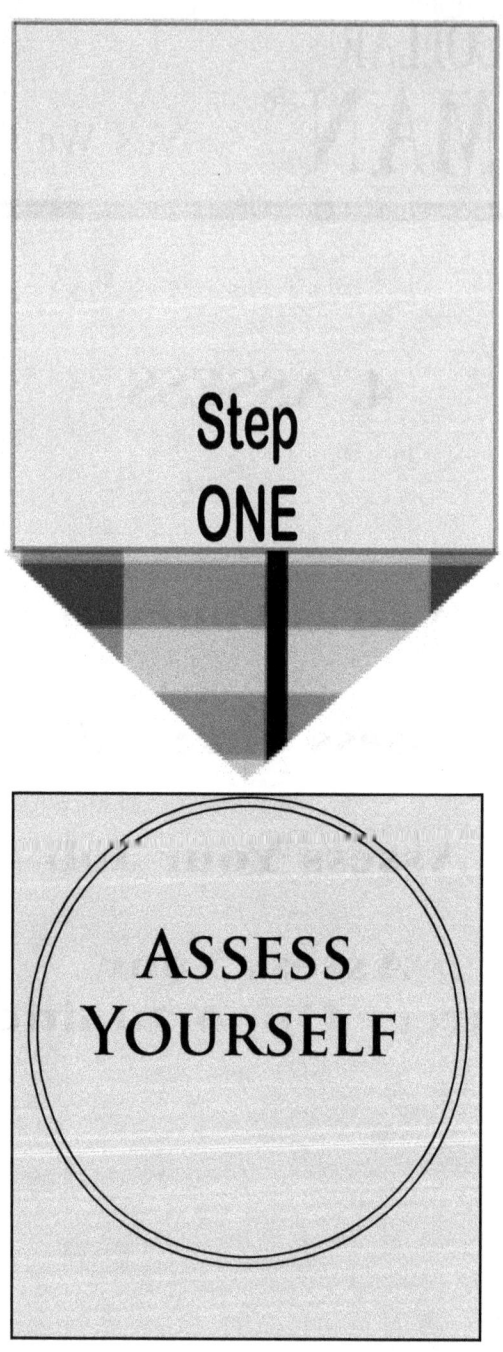

Want a great new job? Are you an entrepreneur? Want a business of your own? ... . What do you like to do? Are you hands on... ... crafts creative? Artistic? like to fix the faucet or decorate the house or sell crafts or hot dogs at the school fair? ... ... What are you passionate about? *(no -- not the Brad Pitt kind of passionate)* Are you Happy? Stressed out? Truly Messed Up?

Who **Are** You?

STEP ONE in creating a new life for yourself is to make sure you know who you are. The better you understand yourself and your needs, d'ruthers, strengths, values, skills and capabilities ... the better chance you will have in creating the kind of new life most likely to give you personal satisfaction.

> You may know yourself well or, like many of us, you may not have had time to explore, in any depth, who you are. There are some techniques, tools and information which can give you a head start. We will talk here about you, the exploration process and some of the ways you can explore YOU.

Why Explore You?

A great part of being happy is to love what you do each day --- job, hobbies, family time and just living. If you can lose yourself in your job, you can be happy. You may not even realize you are happy -- but think about it. Do you love your job? Do you like to do the tasks and activities which make up your work day? Are you good at them? Does it seem like they come naturally to you? Are you focused mainly on those activities, whether mental or physical, without too much worry or thought about family, tonight's dinner, or the vacation trip coming up? That concentration, the natural feel of the activities, the pleasure you get from the little (or bigger) tasks and the focus and concentration you bring to those tasks means that the job is good for you and you love it. Finding a job like that ... one which seems to be made for you ... should be your goal.

The other side of that picture is also true. You may not only be bored - but actually *stressed out* by your job. You may be lost in your job in a different way. You are not living inside your job with that focused concentration and joy which is a true measure of happiness.

You need to understand who you are before you can seek out a job and a life which will make you happy. Money is definitely good! But the old cliche is true -- money cannot buy happiness. (OK -- it will certainly help.) If you can discover who you are, what you like to do and what you are good at doing, then you will have made a tremendous leap toward finding that job meant for you and creating that life which will bring you happiness. Happiness can be wrapped inside a job, i.e. doing something you love to do each day. Remember, your job will essentially BE your life for 40-50 hours a week, 50+ weeks a year.

Some people just seem to 'luck' into a 'great job'. Sometimes those people are just following their natural d'ruthers, as in == hey, I like to do this -- I'll keep on doing it. But, if you explore yourself and understand who you are, then you won't need so much luck. You can search for a job which will take advantage of your natural talents. You can choose that job which seems made for you... ... a job which will make you happy.

Who are YOU?

What makes up YOU, the individual? When we speak of a YOU, what are the parts which we need to explore to truly understand that person. There are three primary aspects of who you are, i.e. the parts which make up a YOU:

The **physical** characteristics of a person can be described by such measures as height and weight. In assessing the physical You in terms of career and life choices, you need to be aware of your personal special capabilities, skills and experiences. You need to identify, explore and assess for yourself those physical characteristics. You know automatically that such factors as an allergy to cats and horses would mean that you probably should not become a veterinarian or vet assistant. What do you need to know about your physical self to make a career choice?

Like the physical self, the **mental** characteristics of a person include capabilities, skills and experience, as well as, innate traits or talents and likes and dislikes. And, of course, the mind and the physical body work together in absorbing and integrating those capabilities and skills. The physical body must support the mind and vice versa. The mental part of you includes your desires, temperament and all those visions and dreams and explosive talents which are the mind.

- Physical
    - Capabilities
    - Skills
    - Experience
- Mental
    - Capabilities
    - Skills
    - Experience
    - Desires
    - Temperament... innate traits
- Spiritual
    - Religious affiliations & beliefs
    - Morality

Mental capabilities may be partially (but only partially) reflected in IQ tests, speed of thought, knowledge base and perhaps, education and other accomplishments. Achievements and drive and innate talents are integral to the mind-body combination which is You. Knowing more about personality and personality types can be helpful here.

Regarding the **spiritual** part of You, we will defer that to others -- like the leaders of your church, your synagogue, or mosque or personal reflections.

> Know yourself and you will be at a place to choose a career and a lifestyle which will satisfy you and make you happy to be who you are and where you are.

The Brain and Who You Are

Our brains are big, complex and wonderful. A human brain begins developing nerve cells (neurons) a little over forty days after conception. Within four months, there are a hundred billion of those little neurons and you will have those same little neurons till late in your life. But here's the extra special thing I did not know (and you may be just as ignorant about this as I was.) Those neurons begin to reach out and talk to each other before you are born. They grow lines or threads (axons) and when an axon touches another brain cell then a communication line is formed, i.e. a synapse. By the time you are three or so, each of those hundred billion axons has formed 12 to 15 thousand connections to other axons (EACH ONE). Like the universe, the complexity and wonders of the brain are hard to imagine. There is a pattern of threads in your brain which is entirely unique to you... ... you alone have that set of brain cells and threads.

However, just like the noise on the internet, the brain begins early to filter out what it needs of these threads and discard the rest. You essentially are setting your personal brain patterns during the first fifteen to sixteen years of your life. Those threads which are not used dissolve and mostly cannot be rebuilt. (There are some instances in learning and memory which do seem to create new synapses, but this is usually a difficult process.)

These brain patterns, i.e. the axon-neuron connections, are the foundation of your personality, your physical and mental abilities, your likes, dislikes, essentially everything about you. So ... ... who you are, as reflected in both your physical and mental world, has a tangible base in your brain. You are you based literally on those patterns of neuron to neuron connections which have been left in your brain from very early in your life. Much of your likes, dislikes, d'ruthers, gifts, talents, abilities are built on those brain patterns, i.e. that pattern of axon-neuron connections which is unique to you.

Wow. Is that fantastic or what?

Self Assessment

Knowing yourself (<u>Step 1</u>: *Assess yourself*.).... should be the basis of any life and career choices you make. Using all the research and information available now on personality types makes this step, assessing yourself, easier. You don't have to just sit in a corner, meditate and chant, *"hoo-rah"*, or something. (Although you can do that if it helps.) What you can do is learn more about personality theories and think about where you fit. Who are you? How do you think, act and react to the world around you? You may elect to consult with a career counselor, either through online interface or in a local office. Or you may want to finish the steps offered here and see how sure you are of your choices at that point.

What steps SHOULD you take to get to know yourself better?
- Think about what you know about yourself already. Who are you? Do you know what you want to do as a career? How strong is that desire? Why?
- What are your strengths, your values, your skills and your knowledge base? Do you work well with your hands; interface and communicate with others; love your own company and maybe like numbers rather than words best? Are you a great soccer or tennis player and love it? What do you know about your SELF?
- Study the information here and online and other information about Values, Skills, Personal Strengths and Personality Types. See what you think as you compare what your learn to what you know about yourself.

- Take some of the free or 'career center' assessment tests. See if they help you know yourself a little better. *Remember: these 'tests' do not provide absolute answers. They are just guides to your thought process.*

Self Assessment Review Topics

There are various tools which can help you learn about yourself. During the self assessment process, you gather and review information about yourself ... as a basis for making a career decision. The self assessment should include:

I. Values. These values describe what is important to you. For example, this might include power, status, independence and autonomy or social interaction.

II. Skills. What are you particularly good at? Are there activities in which you excel? Writing, whitling, painting?

III. Personality. Each of us has patterns of thinking, of loving, of doing and living, and temperaments which are real, which are recognizable and which are consistent from day to day and year to year.

IV. Strengths and Interests. Strengths are your basic talents, what you love and do well -- (i.e. these strengths are based on the patterns in your brain.)

Self Assessment Tips

Knowing that we CAN know ourself is important. Self Assessment should include a close review of your values, strengths and interests, skills and personality. There is now some scientific evidence (quite a lot of research and testing, really) that the self *can* be defined and studied; that, in particular, personality tests and co-relationship studies of career success and personality types are valid.

What does this mean:

1. Each of us has patterns of thinking, of loving, of doing and living. We have temperaments which are real, which are recognizable and which are consistent from day to day and year to year.

2. Building a career on your personal values, your personality and strengths - your basic talents, what you love and do well (i.e. which are based on the patterns in your brain) will mean that you are giving yourself a great foundation for happiness.

3. We can use the tools and information about values, personality, strengths and relationships to careers and we can place some trust in the results.

4. The final decision maker must be you. Does what you learn about yourself, about how that relates to a 'good job' for you, make sense and feel right to you. TRUST YOURSELF ... ... not a test, or a counselor, or a book. YOU! You know how you feel ... You *know* who you are. If the test answers or advice feels wrong -- start again. It IS wrong.

You should not try to make any one of these categories, e.g. personality type, the only factor, or even, perhaps, the major factor in your choice of a career. Just like any other single point in such a decision process, you need to consider everything. Your father and your mother or other family members may already have a plumbing business and you have been considering joining them. Just because your personality type is not specifically correlated to success in the plumbing trades does not mean that you should not go ahead with plumbing as a career. However, it does mean that you should consider how you will fit yourself into the role, using what you know about your personality. Can you do the job and will you like doing it? You will need to anticipate any accommodations you may have to make to do the job.

Use what is discussed in this chapter about theories, testing and tools to help you in assessing and understanding yourself. Follow up on some of the references. Take a look at some of the relevant books and internet websites. Find out for yourself what is out there to help you understand yourself. Spend some time on this. Spend as much time as you can reasonably spare on this first part of your life change process.

Remember that understanding yourself as well as possible is key to everything else. Then, either see a career counselor (and, keep in mind, depending on your finances and circumstances, you may be able to find some free local support.) Or, if you elect not to see a career counselor, then read as much as you can stand from the internet and books. Take some of the personal assessment tests which are available on the internet. Some of the books, like the <u>NOW, Discover your Strengths</u> (Buckingham and Clifton) have codes in the book which will allow you access to some of their self tests. There are also some excellent free self tests for values, interests, and personality types online - and, of course, available through a career counselor. The Myers-Briggs Personality Type Indicator® is one of the tests most used by career and other counselors.

Read the material, think about yourself and your d'ruthers and talents and personality patterns. Analyze some of the test results. Understand yourself a little better. Then revisit and rethink and re-process ... as you jump into the next steps of assessing your job and your life.

I. Self Assessment: *Values*

Everyone has values. But what are values? Values help to guide you in living your life. Values are those deeply held convictions and constraints which help us to live within our own standards and ideals. They are based on strong personal beliefs which have been gained through such influences as culture, family teachings, and personal experiences. These values guide your behavior and keep you on a path of living which is acceptable to you.

The word 'value' is derived from the Latin 'valeo', to be strong. Values are based on core beliefs which do essentially make us 'strong' and shape who we are as unique individuals. Understanding your values is important when choosing a career. Your values include, for example, your sense of fair play and honesty, your love of independence or your need to be a part of a team. If you don't consider your values when planning your career, you may end up not happy with your choice. For example, someone who needs to have independence and autonomy in her work would not be happy in a job where every action is decided by someone else.

History

Plato thought and wrote about values in the Greece of twenty four hundred years ago. He studied values as concepts which define virtuous living. He defined some of the values which he believed his people should live by, e.g. courage, justice, happiness, knowledge, and truthfulness.

In the 1930's, a psychologist, **Gordon Allport**, studied values from a different perspective, i.e. as essential links to how we live. He defined a list of what he called traits, which are esssentially what we are naming *values*. He described these as easily recognized consistencies in a person's life that are unique to that individual. These are the 'traits' which define a life. During that period, values were an active study topic in the field of psychology. The Journal of Abnormal Psychology published a list of seventy six values and others were added to that list over the next 20-30 years.

Later, Milton Rokeach (<u>The Nature of Human Values</u>) defined values as 'an enduring belief that a specific mode of conduct ... is personally and socially preferable to alternative modes.' He published a list of what he called 'intrumental' and 'terminal' values. Instrumental values he defined as those which help you determine how to behave, e.g. self controlled, logical, independent, forgiving. Terminal values are those which are the goals of living, e.g. friendship, love, self respect. He developed the Rokeach Value Survey which includes ranking the relative importance of each value in his lists of eighteen 'instrumental' and eighteen 'terminal' values. This survey is still used today.

Abraham Maslow, in the 1960's, described the role of values in a person's inner decision-making process. In particular, Maslow studied decisions regarding self actualization, i.e. developing one's full potential. Maslow felt that good values motivate a person to get where she wants to go. He felt that, rather than immutable life factors, people can *choose* some of their values. He believed that some values produce more positive benefits than others. He observed that self actualizing values produce more confidence, joy and passion in living -- what he considered a more 'healthy' individual.

Since the 1980's, researchers have tried to reach some consensus on the most important values. There are some basic lists of values. However, there are literally hundreds of values which have been identified over the years of study. A few examples of values which have been identified and described are: *adventure, balance, confidence, creativity, control, self discipline, order, faith, autonomy, spirituality, honesty, wisdom, hope, growth, knowledge, self reliance, compassion, power, fun, freedom, forgiveness.*

Some recent research has focused on finding out what values shape a person's life, what it is that makes some people function well, achieve success and become personally fulfilled. The researchers are also searching for those core values which are consistent across cultures and time - i.e. 'signature human strengths'. There is some belief that there are core values which are valid across time and cultures -- e.g. wisdom, courage, humanity, justice, temperance, and transcendence. Values are the result of culture, training, environment and inherent individual characteristics. There is also some belief now that values can be specifically taught, e.g. kindness and generosity.

Why Values are important

Career counselors and psychologists agree that values are primary motivators of behavior. They say that a person will be happier and healthier when the individual motivation comes from a well defined set of individual core values. If you understand your own values, your own value priorities, then your life choices will be much more clear. The lifestyle you desire can be defined in terms of those values and value priorities. If you value friendship highly, (or, perhaps, team work) then you will work hard to keep your friends. You will want to work closely together and respect and work within the framework of your team. If you value helpfulness (service) highly, then you could achieve personal satisfaction from a life of service, such as nursing or teaching. If independence and autonomy are important values for you, then you will find more satisfaction in careers which give you independence of thought and action.

You will be most happy if you clearly understand your values and choose a career and make other life choices based on what you know about your own values. You may have to make choices based on prioritizing your values - since having everything is not usually possible. Prestige, great pay, a chance to serve others, independence and no risk ... those are all values which you may know are important to you. However, you may have to decide whether prestige or pay or service are of most value.

Values and Assessment

Family, friendship, teamwork, fun, independence, autonomy, authority, self discipline, service, structure, duty, wisdom, moderation, leadership, spirituality, influence, power, humility, comfort, stability, aesthetics (artistic expression)

Those are just a few more examples of the values which may define your life and be of importance in selecting a career.

There are a number of self assessment value inventories (*e.g. Minnesota Importance Questionnaire, Survey of Interpersonal Values, Temperament and Values inventory.*) A values inventory will ask you to answer questions like - Is it important to you to interact with people? or Is a high rate of pay important to you. In some of these, you may be given a list of 'values' and asked to choose and prioritize those values which are most importalt to you in your job.

Think about your own values. Research. Take a look at some of the more complete lists of values and develop your own priority list for use in choosing your career.

II. Self Assessment: *Skills*

Skills are those things which you do - e.g. write, analyze, add-subtract-multiply, listen, throw a baseball. You may have skills that you love, things that gather and focus your energy and bring you joy. These are your strengths and more time is devoted to those strengths as section IV in this chapter. Those strengths play a large role in achieving joy and passion in your life. You may have a skill without the passion for doing that particular 'thing'. All your skills are important. Whether you love them or just have learned the skill and have some experience in that arena -- those skills are part of you. An employer will be interested in what you can do. Skills are categorized by the US Department of Labor as: Skills with ideas; skills with people; and, skills with things. Some career counselors divide skills into work related general categories:

- Basic Work Skills - communication, reading, writing, thinking, mathematics, learning strategies, time management.
- Technical Skills - skills which are specific to a particular career, e.g. using specific equipment, project management and scheduling, carpentry.
- Interpersonal Skills - interacting with other people with proficiency. Listening, understanding, making yourself understood, likeability, creating a productive work environment.

Most important skills to employers

There was a survey of employers in 2005 by the National Association of Colleges and Employers (NACE), in which employers rated the most desired employee skills. The skills most in demand were:

- Communication
- Teamwork
- Analytical
- Interpersonal
- Computer
- Organizational
- Leadership

Of course, in the Blue Collar skilled trades careers, an employer is going to especially value your hands-on skills specific to your craft.

Skills Assessment

You may take skills self assessment tests to further your understanding of self. Most of these are inventories which help you list and describe what kinds of skills you posess. During the process, you should think about which of those skills you wish to pursue and enhance. *(See in Section IV of this chapter just how skills, talents and strenths are related.)*

III. Self Assessment: *Personality*

The third category for assessment of Self is Personality and Personality Types. Much of the extensive bank of information (including books, internet, other media) on understanding your personality, your SELF and others is based on the Myers/Briggs and Jung's Personality Theories and Personality Types.

Jung is a key figure in the field of personality research. He was born in Switzerland in 1875 and died in 1961. He was a contemporary of Freud and of Myers. Much of his work is seminal, that is, he planted the seeds. Jung remains an important figure in the field of psychology today. Much of his work had to do with psychosexual development, and the conscious, preconscious and unconscious. He wrote about the id, the ego and the super-ego. Jung is a super person to study. He was a prolific writer and many of his ideas were unique and still unmatched by any thinker, psychologist or otherwise.

Jung is one of my personal heroes. He stressed the importance of individual rights in a person's relation to the state and society, as well as, other political, religious, and relationship arenas and he felt that there are some simple human truths. (He was courageously against the Nazis.) He is best known now for his works: <u>Psychology of the Unconscious</u> (1912) and <u>Psychological Types</u> (1921). He founded a new school of psychotherapy, called analytical psychology or Jungian psychology.

Myers and Briggs extrapolated their own *brand* of Personality Type theory from Jung's writings in his book Psychological Types. The Myers-Briggs Type Indicator (MBTI) assessment is a psychometric questionnaire designed to measure psychological preferences in how people perceive the world and make decisions. Essentially, this is the basis for the current Personality Type field of work which we suggest for assessment of self. This can be a foundation for choosing a career you like, can do well, and which may make you happy.

The original developers of the personality inventory were Katharine Cook Briggs and her daughter, Isabel Briggs Myers. They began creating the indicator during World War II (Jung was a contemporary.) They believed that they could help women who were entering the workforce for the first time to identify the sort of jobs where they would feel comfortable and be able to do the jobs. The Myers-Briggs Personality Type Indicator® has been taken by millions of people. Results have been researched, documented and refined.

The initial questionnaire which grew into the Myers-Briggs Type Indicator®, was first published in 1962. The MBTI 'focuses on normal populations and emphasizes the value of naturally occurring differences.' CPP Inc., the publisher of the MBTI instrument, calls it "the world's most widely used personality assessment", with as many as two million assessments administered annually.

Personality Types

Personality types have been studied, defined, and validated by numerous researchers. These personality types appear to be a valid way to evaluate your own personality and choose a career. Researchers have identified, described and studied eight different aspects, i.e. traits, of personality. These are the characteristics people use to communicate, to interact, to organize, work, solve problems and make decisions.

There are a number of personality theories, tools and tests, including the Myers-Briggs personality Type Indicator®. This *test* is really an inventory -- no right and wrong answers. It is just a set of questions which allow for developing a psychological profile of the person. These personality concepts and tools provide an excellent starting point for beginning the process of understanding yourself.

The four faces of personality.

Each person has some mix of each of the 'opposing' traits shown.

> External energy:::Internal energy
> Sensing:::Intuitive
> Thinking:::Feeling
> Judging:::Perceiving

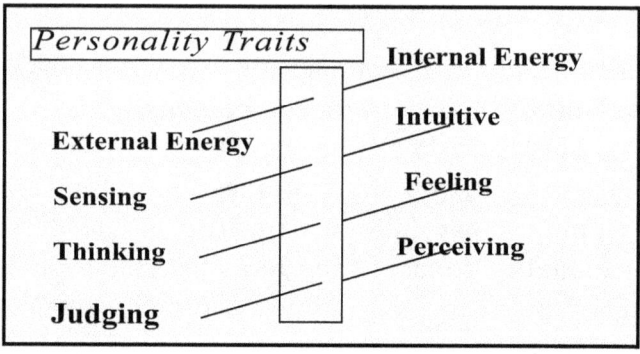

Rather than 'opposing' personality traits, however, each of these is really a continuum of these traits within the same person. When you take a personality inventory, like the Myers-Briggs personality type indicator®, the results characterize your personality by letters designating the results. What is the most dominant in these four sets of traits? Thus a person may be said to be an INTJ --- Internal, iNtuitive, Thinking, Judging. Those are the personality traits which are dominant (at least to some greater or lesser extent) for that person. That appears to be how she views and reacts to the world.

There are sixteen combinations of these personality traits and each of these has been researched extensively.

ISTJ; ISFJ; INFJ; INTJ; ISTP; ISFP; INFP; INTP; ESTP; ESFP; ENFP; ENTP; ESTJ; ESFJ; ENFJ; ENTJ

Because millions of people have taken these tests and correlations have been made with career success, they can be used with some reliability in career guidance. As I mentioned before, you may wish to take one of these brief introductory tests on line or go into a local career counselor/office and take the more intensive testing and get more career guidance. Whatever approach you decide to use, take a look at the introduction here. You can learn a lot about yourself just by applying these notes to your own understanding of your personality.

Extrovert vs Introvert

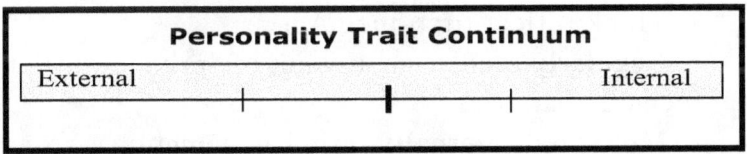

Are you an extrovert or an introvert. Each person gets energy and may live best in the external world and/or their own internal world. That external world is a world of other people and activities outside themselves. The internal world is focused on inner thoughts, personal interests and creativity.

Each person lives in both worlds - the internal and the external. These are complementary sides of the personality. But each of us is more directed towards the outer world or towards the inner world of our own thoughts and imagination.

> *In this section - the characteristics shown are from the website: www.PersonalityPathways.com. Go to their website for more. Thanks to those authors for the information.*

Some of the characteristics of <u>Extroverted personalities</u> are:
- Act first, think/reflect later
- Feel deprived when cutoff from interaction with the outside world
- Usually open to and motivated by outside world of people and things
- Enjoy wide variety and change in people relationships

Some of the characteristics of <u>Introverted Personalities</u> are that they:
- Think/reflect first, then Act
- Regularly require an amount of "private time" to recharge batteries
- Motivated internally, mind is sometimes so active it is "closed" to outside world
- Prefer one-to-one communication and relationships

Take a look at yourself. Can you see your place on the personality profile? Are you an extrovert or an introvert, by nature?

Sensing vs iNtuitive

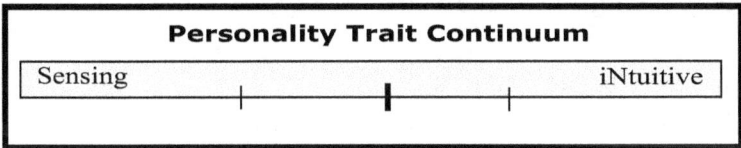

The sensing person notices the sights, sounds, smells and all the details of the present. This person's brain automatically categorizes, organizes and records and stores the specifics from the here and now. It is reality based, dealing with 'what is.' This sensory brain remembers specific details from the past. On the opposite of this personality trait continuum, the Intuitive (N) personality seeks to understand, interpret and form total picture patterns from the myriad of details collected by the brain. The Intuitive side of the brain collects and records those patterns and relationships. This intuitive side of the brain allows for and automatically looks for the possibilities of the now and the future. It is conceptual and deals in abstract thinking.

Most of us think and perceive in a range across this personality continuum. (Descriptions are shown in www.PersonalityPathways.com) However, each person instinctively favors one end of this spectrum. See if you can decide where you fit.

Sensing Characteristics
• Mentally lives in the Now, attending to present opportunities
• Uses common sense. Creating practical solutions is automatic/instinctual
• Memory recall is rich in detail of facts and past events

- Improvises from past experience
- Likes clear and concrete information; dislikes guessing when facts are "fuzzy"

Intuitive Characteristics
- Mentally lives in the Future, attending to future possibilities
- Uses imagination and creating/inventing new possibilities is automatic-instinctual
- Memory recall emphasizes patterns, contexts, and connections
- Improvises from theoretical understanding
- Comfortable with ambiguous, fuzzy data and with guessing its meaning.

Note: Thanks to www.PersonalityPathways.com for this information. Go to their website for more.

Are you a sensing kind of personality or would you class yourself as an intuitive?

Thinking vs Feeling

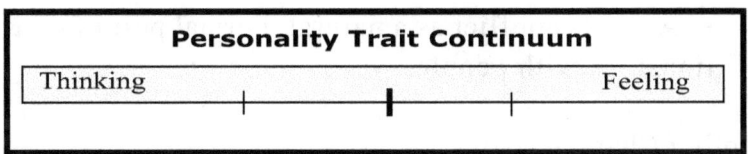

What is your 'automatic' way of making judgments and choices?

This personality trait is a continuum between the THINKING side of the brain which analyzes information objectively and the FEELING side of the brain which makes decisions based on likes/dislikes already formed, human variables. If your decisions are more usually based on facts and deductions based on those facts, then you should place yourself in the THINKING part of the continuum. If you usually make decisions on how you feel about the people and the situation...... what the impact will be, then your subjective nature is dominant.

Again .... there is no right or wrong answer here. And, in fact, people use both sides of their nature ... subjective and logical ... to make decisions and judgments.

However, we each have a natural inclination to one or the other, especially when decisions or judgments must be made quickly and/or with conflicting or little information.

Thinking Personality Characteristics
- Instinctively search for facts and logic in a decision situation.
- Naturally notices tasks and work to be accomplished.

- Easily able to provide an objective and critical analysis.
- Accepts conflict as a natural, normal part of relationships with people.

Feeling Characteristics
- Instinctively employs personal feelings and impacts on people in decision situations
- Naturally sensitive to people needs and reactions.
- Naturally seek consensus and popular opinions.
- Unsettled by conflict; have almost a toxic reaction to disharmony.

Note: Thanks again to www.PersonalityPathways. com for this information. Go to their website for more.

How do you think you usually make your judgments and decisions? Are you a T or and F?

Judging vs Perceiving

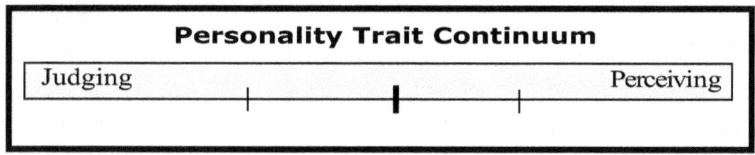

How do you usually act and interact with the outside world?

Each person must make decisions and manage her/his life by gathering information, thinking and organizing those thoughts and making decisions and taking action and interacting with the external world. If you are naturally on the Judging end of this continuum for interaction with the external world, then you most often have a plan for the interaction. You want to be prepared, organize the world around you, set goals and reach them and move on. At the Perceiving end of this continuum, you will take the outside world 'as it comes'. You do not do a lot of planning for the everyday interactions with the world. You adapt to the situations and are open to whatever opportunities arise with flexibility.

Judging Characteristics
- Plan many of the details in advance before moving into action.
- Focus on task-related action; complete meaningful segments before moving on.
- Work best and avoid stress when able to keep ahead of deadlines.
- Naturally use targets, dates and standard routines to manage life.

Perceiving Characteristics
- Comfortable moving into action without a plan; i.e. plan on-the-go.
- Like to multitask, have variety, mix work and play.
- Naturally tolerant of time pressure; work best close to the deadlines.
- Instinctively avoid commitments which interfere with flexibility, freedom and variety

How do you see yourself?   Judging (J) or Perceiving (P)?

Remember, your answers should be based on how you automatically react to daily life and situations and how you live your life among others.

IV. Self Assessment:
Strengths based Psychology

The next category for your self assessment exercise is called Strengths-based Psychology. Donald O. Clifton (1924-2003) is described as the Father of Strengths-Based Psychology and creator of the Clifton StrengthsFinder®. He has been honored by the American Psychological Association for his fifty years of work in Strengths-based psychology. The Gallop Organization uses these strengths-based theories in their management consulting practice. You will find offshoots of both strengths and personality type groups in your research and personal assessment process.

Go with Your Strengths

As with the Personality Types, the strengths consultants talk about the enduring and unique nature of each person's strengths. In their book, NOW, Discover your Strengths, Buckingham and Clifton discuss personal strengths and building on those strengths. They say that your greatest room for growth is in the areas of your greatest strengths. There is a huge amount of information available on Strengths assessment and putting those strengths to work for you.

What are Strengths?

Talents, Knowledge and Skills

Here's some brief notes about the Strengths field in the

> - Talents
>   Patterns of thought, feeling, behavior
>
> - Knowledge
>   Facts/Content
>
> - Skills
>   Structured Knowledge
>   Experience

Personality arena: Talents are your naturally occurring patterns of thought, feeling, or behavior. (from <u>Now, Discover your Strengths</u> -- by Marcus Buckingham and Donald O Clifton) Knowledge, they write, consists of the facts and lessons learned. Skills involve the structured knowledge, ie. steps of an activity. These three combine to create your strengths. The best way to build on your strengths is to find and identify your dominant talents -- then refine them with knowledge and skills. **For this reason, you should seek knowledge and skills to enhance your talents.** Although many people say to work on your weaknesses, Buckingham and Clifton write that you should find your talents and go for them. Don't divert your energy and time ... where your talents lie are where your greatest returns will be achieved.

So how do they say that you can identify your talents?

Step back and watch yourself. Observe for yourself how quickly you pick up a new activity. Do you become absorbed to such an extent that you lose track of time. Try another activity after awhile and watch again. You can see which you do best almost automatically and which you like the most.

Dominant talents will show themselves. You can look over your past and probably pick some out for yourself. You either like and are good at playing ball or speaking or building a cabinet or nurturing a garden. The more you use a talent, the greater your strength in that area will become. The Skill and Knowledge that you acquire will, of course, make you better. Skill and Knowledge which comes from experience and education will also apply to those things which you do that are not Talents. But these counselors emphasize that you will never be as good in those areas where you have no innate Talent -- and you will not love to do that activity, i.e. the one which is not based on your innate brain patterns. All that fits with our understanding of brain development and unique patterns of brain activity.

So what are talents? Can we name some so that we can begin to apply this to our own analysis? Are you imaginative, assertive, precise, persistent, tactful, empathetic, witty, verbal, cooperative, dominant, ambitious. There are a lot of these Talents or Personality Traits which could be described. Confident, thoughtful, artistic, dexterous.

Recognizing your Strengths

In the book, <u>NOW, Discover Your Strengths,</u> the au-

- Spontaneous Reactions
- Yearnings
- Rapid Learning
- Satisfactions

thors say that there are four indications and ways to recognize a strength:

1. Your spontaneous reactions to a situation: How do you react, say, to an emergency? Do you take charge; do you flee? How do you act automatically to any given situation.

2. Yearnings -- You really want to do something -- like paint or dance. Especially at a young age. Your daughter is already going to dance classes and loving it, at 5 years old.

3. Rapid Learning -- sometimes an activity just seems to be YOU. You might not have even known that you could be good at it; but when you try it -- WOW. You can do it like a pro.

4. Satisfactions --- you do it -- you love it.

One of the tools used here is something developed by these consultants -- called the Strengths Finder Profile. This is an inventory -- a list of questions with two answers -- which is supposed to help you 'sharpen your perceptions'. You can find a code to access this profiler -- on the book cover of the NOW, Discover Your Strengths book. (*Note: No. Unfortunately I have no financial interests in the book.*)

Personality Types and Careers

Personality types and, to some extent, strengths and values, have been shown to have some relationship to career choices and to career success. It is certainly good to know about them and also to know what the research appears to have shown about these career relationships. My major concern is that you do not take this information as your primary and sole guide in the selection of a career. If you go down the avenue of taking all the personality tests, finding out your *'personality type'*, and getting the related career choice information, that is all great. However, you do need to take it in ONLY as another source for your analysis of YOU.

What does your gut (for want of another term) say to you. What do you really want to do? What is your d'ruthers choice. Listen to your SELF, your wants, your cares, your innate abilities. Get acquainted with the information and find out as much as you can about yourself. Then make your decision based, not on tests and experts, but on your own self knowledge. What do you know about yourself ... inside yourself?

More information ...

I've included more from the experts about the research and relationships between Personality Types and Career Choice and Career Success in Appendix C.

Keep in mind: no one
(NO ONE)
thinks this information includes a guarantee of success or failure in your chosen career. But, it might help you make your decision. So take it and use it. Fold it into the rest of the data you collect to make a career choice.

So -- take off!!!

Go ... ...

Assess Yourself!!!

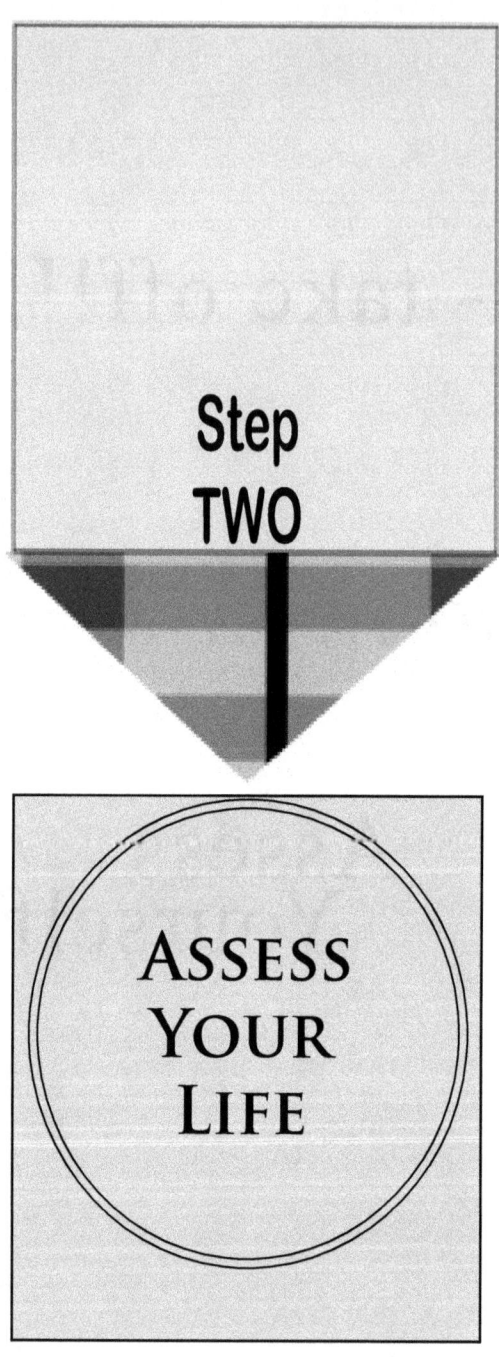

Step TWO

Assess Your Life

Your life includes everything about you ... who you are, who and what you surround yourself with, what is your job, what are your *outside-the-job* activities and cares. It includes all aspects integral to you: Family. Social. Educational. Career. Financial. Residential and physical environment. Spiritual. Personal. Health. Fun and Recreation. Safety/legal issues.

Are you satisfied with your life?

Who decides what your life will be? What your life is now?

YOU

Independent Women with Confidence

The Decision Maker in your Life

You are the decision maker in your life. YOU decide whether you will ride the winds of circumstance and necessity which have been forced on you. YOU decide if you will change your life... ... grasp more enjoyment and satisfaction from each moment of that life.

That sounds pretty much craziness, doesn't it? We all know that with children and a family AND a job AND myriad responsibilities of a full and sometimes overpowering life --- We can be swept along willy nilly with just living. However, we certainly can make some decisions. Do we stack the dishes in the sink for later or do we make kitchen clean-up a singalong family affair? So ... ... **Yes** --- Actually we do. We may feel forced by circumstances, but mostly life is determined by a series of small to larger decisions each of us makes about the next action or inaction we take each day. Consciously or not. Will you go pick up the twins from school every day or is it too much to ask your mother or father or Jane, down the street, to make some regular school runs for you? Do you have that argument with your significant other or wait 'til another day.

How do you get the most of out of your life at this moment. In order to make life the best that it can be each moment, we need to know what our ideal life style means. For this exercise, we will set aside the time spent in a job. We will discuss your total life **outside of work.**

What makes you happy? What do you do outside work hours which gives you the most satisfaction? Are you so wound up in responsibilities and routine that you do not have even two

hours a week which could be yours alone?
If you had two hours a day, or even two hours a week for yourself, what would you do? Would doing that make you happy?

There are a number of *must* steps in creating the best life you can be living.

- Know who you are
- Explore your life ... discover yourself in your life
- Decide what you want from your life; how do you want to live
- Plan on change if you need it
- Start now to change it

The first step in creating a new life for yourself is to make sure you know and understand the life you are living. What are the various aspects and characteristics of that life. What are the activities and tasks you must attend to each day. You need to explore what those are, understand fully what is happening to you, with you, and through you on a daily basis. Then you can make some decisions about what you want your life to be like. What you will need to do to transform it into a more satisfying place for you to be ... ... i.e. your life .... for YOU.

Components of your Life

The many sides of your life include the physical, spiritual, intellectual; the emotional, social and financial. We can examine these parts as separate entities. We know what the words mean.

>Physical -- Health, personal body, well being
>Spiritual -- Belief systems and core strengths & values
>Intellectual -- Mental agility, learning capabilities, mental strength

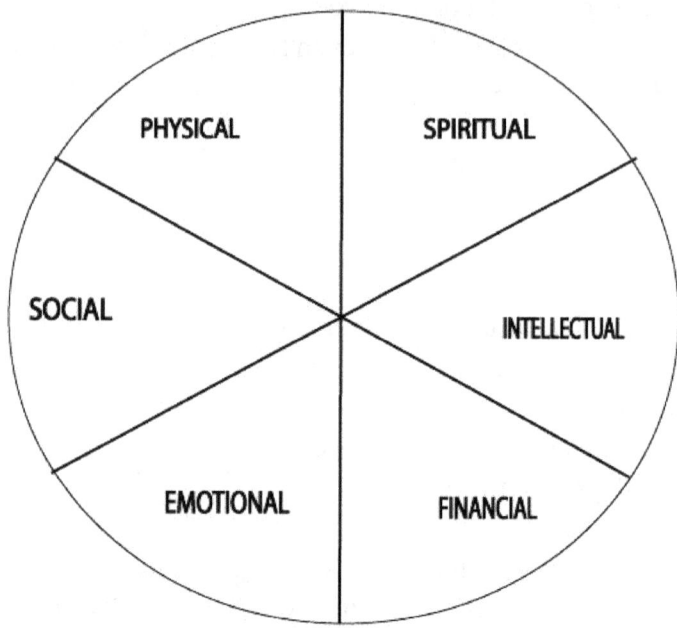

Social -- Communications and people relationships and support systems

Emotional -- General attitude toward life, self and the external world

Financial -- Assets and income to provide life necessities and desires for self and family

Taking a MY LIFE Inventory

Those are the components which make up your life. We will gather them into four different areas and take a 'My Life' inventory. If the goal is to make some decisions about your job, then you need to also understand the other aspects of your life and how those impact your job. Changing your job will mean training, transition and major upheavals. Now is the time to analyze the impact areas in the remainder of your life. What can be changed? What must be changed? Take a look at each of these arenas and think about your life. Review these 'how I live' areas and highlight those which must change if you change your job... your career. As you review, you may even decide to rate yourself, your life, the choices you have made and the results which are reflected in your own life right now?

Your Physical Environment

Home -- Where do you live?
Do you like it/love it? What do you like about it? What do you not like about it? This should include everything from the physical components, like the fireplace in the living room to the fact that there are only two bedrooms and you really need three. This should also call up a question of how do you feel when you drive up to the house/apartment? How does walking in the door make you feel? Do you feel some of the stress already falling from your shoulders... ... 'this is home' and I'm comfortable and safe now?

Furniture
Yeah -- kind a lame thing to add to your ratings list, right? But --- do you need a desk or work area for any new education/schooling requirements? And, actually, I find that the great rocking chair and the contemporary teak side tables in my living room draw me into their embrace over and over again. I love those 'things'. I absolutely know that I could live without the 'things'. But they sure make my life a little jot more worth living .. just looking at them and being there inside that safe cocoon of familiarity and comfort.

Auto/Transportation
Do you have transportation which is reliable and comfortable? 'nough said here, I think.

Location/geography
Do you live in a location geographically that you like? Do you want to be in Florida or Alaska and you are now in Wisconsin? or the opposite? A big city vs a small, rural community?

Home/living status/environment
Is your home in a 'good' location? Rate the schools. Parks. Convenience to work and school and church/mosque/synagogue? Traffic and Noise and convenience to shopping, etc.

Emotional and Social Well Being

> *Review your laugh meter. Have you laughed out loud at least once a day over the past week?*

Personal
Are you generally happy with yourself? Upbeat...positive? How about your physical appearance? Working on something like weight? What are you clothes like? Do you have 'work clothes' and play clothes? Enough? What would you need for school, a new job?

Family and Friends
Do you have a partner whom you trust and love ... who will stand by you and help you through the difficult times and share the good ones with pleasure? Do you have parents and siblings and other family living close by? Are you on good terms, enjoy their company and they want the best for you? Do you have a few close personal friends living nearby? This means the difference between having a support system and having to create one. What is a support system? You need someone to talk to, to tell your dreams and cry with at your stumbles? You need someone to take the kids to school if you can't make it. You need a support system to just goof off and drain away

the stress which is a natural part of living ... and, more so, if you decide on a career change.

Time, freedom
How much time do you have for yourself? Do you have three kids and a partner who works also? Is someone always expecting you to be somewhere at specific times? Think about how you will manage if you try to incorporate more activities into an already busy schedule.

Pets
Do you have pets? or delicate plants? Both of which need careful, regular care. Factor in their care.

Computer
You may need a computer for school or other training... for job search ... for correspondence. This may not be critical but think about it. Do you have one? What will you do for these needs if they come up?

Financial Circumstances

Stable, regular income
Do you have a regular source of money which is not tied to your job? Do you have a partner who works and who will stand by you... makes enough so that you could be out of work for awhile? If not, can you make arrangements to live with parents or have some temporary support from a loved ones? You may need to address this sooner, rather than later, in the *change your job; change you life* process.

Assets
Do you have savings or a home or other salable goods which you could tap as a 'tide you over' source of income?

Budget
Do you live on a budget and generally stick to it? You really need to think about drafting one for current expenses and what you would need on a regular basis if you made a change. This could be just a listing of money coming in and expenses, i.e. regular outgo, and what you have coming in. ... ... It sounds simple and frequently turns into stress and headaches. But ... ... you need to understand up front what the reality is. This activity will clarify the reality of your finances for you. (If you needed any clarification.)

Insurance and Fall Back
Health insurance will be particularly important and may be particularly difficult .. if you leave one job before jumping into the next. What will you do? Auto and home insurance and other such bills will continue.

Health and Well Being

Do you think mostly people are mean and out to get you? ...that things almost never go your way? *or* Are most of the people around you good and fun to be around? Like Will Rogers -- 'I never met a man I didn't like!'. Who you are and your attitude toward life is reflected in the answers to these questions. You physical and your mental health are joined and one impacts the other.

Personal
Inventory your health. Both mental and physical. Are you generally physically well? How old are you? Do you have any chronic conditions? Take care of them and yourself. Should you be anticipating health issues based on genetic factors, like your mother had this and so you need to check to make sure no signs for you. Are you frequently depressed without having a reason? Ask someone who knows you if you can't assess this aspect of yourself.

With the changes in medicine, doctors can help you with this these days. Go see a doctor if you haven't done so in over a year and especially if there appears to be something which is 'bugging' you.

Family Health
Assess your kids and you partner's physical and mental health in the same way you do your own. Get some regular check ups, if needed. Make sure you have a family doctor and that s/he follows you and your family and gives you the support you need.

Health Factors and Habits
Nutrition, exercise, adequate sleep and rest. Those are all factors which you should inventory for yourself and your family. Now might be the time to make any changes which you know are necessary to stay healthy on a long term basis.

What is your Career Change Realism Quotient?

Give yourself a realistic assessment of your life --- as it relates to your ability to make a major change in careers. What life changes will you need to change based on what you know about a career transition?

Go back over each area and decide whether you can manage a career change within the parameters of your current life. Can you change your life enough to fit your living around a career change?

Be practical in your assessment. Don't beat yourself up if you decide you cannot do this right now. If you can't, you can't. You don't want to regret your decision later.

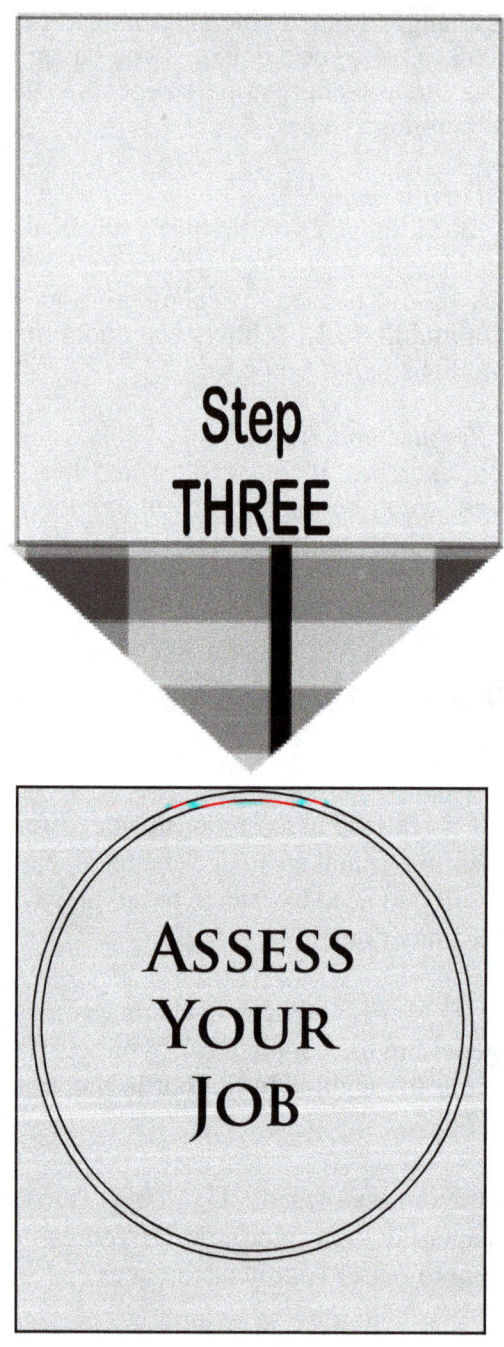

Do you love your job?

Do you Hate Your JOB?

Do you hate your job with a passion?

Know when to fold'em

How do you know if you should change your career -- go on to a new job? The best way to know when to change your job is the simplest. You just cannot stand going to work anymore. *and/OR* You cannot support yourself and your family on the money you make.

Why Assess your Job?

You have probably made your 'gut level' decision about changing your career and leaving your job. You can't stand it, you don't like it, you hate it --- you don't make enough money --- or maybe you just got laid off and you are sure you don't want to find another job like the last one. So, why should you bother with analyzing that old job?

That 'old job' and how you feel about it is going to tell you a lot about what your new job should be. Not just for you, the person, but for you and the life you want to live. What aspects of the job were good, really good for you? Is it close to where you live? Is there child care? So even if you have decided to go for a career change, analyze the 'old job'. That will tell you much about what you need in a new job. You should also be revisiting your 'gut level' decision. Don't forget to think about what you might do differently in order to better fit into your current job and, maybe, make it better for yourself. Also, as you go through each point, think about how this does or, maybe, should impact your decision about career change. The key is -- and what a cliche this is --- but, here goes:

THINK OUTSIDE the BOX.

While you are assessing this current job, be evaluating again your decision to leave it and tackle something new.

Jobs:
How to Assess

Think about your current job. What do you like? What do you find unacceptable? What would you look for in your perfect job? How do you decide what you like; what you don't like? What would you like to see in any new job? Rate your current job and be thinking about what you want in something new.

The most basic aspects of any job are:

1. Do you like doing what you are doing?
2. Do you make enough money to support you, your family and your desired lifestyle.

How do you feel about the job ... the work, itself?

Do you mostly enjoy the tasks and activities which are part of your job? For example, if you are dealing with customers and handling telephone calls, do you like talking with the people and handling the issues which arise? Is it essentially boring? Do you have trouble staying awake? Think about this. Review for yourself what happens ... on a regular basis -- don't count those times where you just did not get enough sleep last night.

Are you passionate about the goals and achievements and, basically, the regular work? If not passionate, how would you rate your involvement and joy in the work. Assume 'passion' is at the ten level -- rate the job for yourself and your interest. Anything less than a 5 and you really need to think seriously about 'fold-n' em'.

How do you feel about the people?

Do you work directly with people whom you like? Do you feel comfortable with them? If your job is related to others -- are the people good to work with? Do they do their jobs well and make it easy for you to do yours?

If you interact with customers for some major portion of your day ---- do you like it? Do you enjoy the people? ... or Do you find yourself, for example, stressed out with the customer issues and interface?

Is there some team spirit? Does the group work together, get together occasionally for a 'beer/softdrink after work' or a birthday party at mid day? Are they fun to be around?

Rate your job from 1 to 10 on the people you have to work with or be around each day?

Location and work environment

How close do you live to your job? Is there a long commute? Do you ride public transportation? How good is the commute? How short or long?

Is the job location in a good neighborhood? Do you feel safe walking to/from your car or bus? Is it a pleasant place to be?

Rate your job location on a scale of 1 to 10.

How about the physical environment/your workplace. Is it a large, drafty warehouse -- filled with rats and cold weather? or is the temperature great ... the surroundings pleasing? The major thing with physical environment is your comfort and safety levels.

Rate your physical environment on a 1 to 10 basis.

Financial Rewards

Do you make enough money to meet your living necessities, other needs, and savings? Do you make enough to satisfy your wants -- what you want -- not just your relative comfort level. (Reverse this question a little and ask yourself if what you 'want' is realistic.) Are the financial rewards commensurate with the work that you do? Are you paid about what others are paid for the same job, i.e. the market rate in your geographical area for the work that you do?

One of the most critical issues here is -- do you make enough money to support yourself and your family reasonably well? If not, then this is a 'make or break' issue. This could be the factor which will swing your decision to change jobs.

How do you rate your financial rewards? 1 to 10 ?

Other Rewards

Are there some extenuating circumstances which make the job more positive or negative and which have nothing to do with the work itself or the finances? Perhaps it is a family business or maybe they have a child care center and you can not work without such a facility. You may need to reconsider the extra benefits you receive and weigh those against your personal rewards from the job.

There may be other ways you can satisfy some of the special needs which the extra rewards satisfy. Consider how you would handle that. You may unwillingly be forced to make a change. You may find that you just can not continue to work at a job which you hate.

How do you rate the other rewards from the job? 1 to 10?

Skills, Training, and Experience requirements and utilization

How much training was required to obtain your current position? How much experience do you have in this job? Are special skills required? Part of the evaluation here concerns your level of authority and responsibility and whether you are willing to give up some level of current status. Are you willing to go back to an elementary level and essentially begin again? Will the job satisfaction and financial rewards quickly make up for such a change. A primary goal here is to recognize the issue and to allow for your distress, depending on how important this is to you.

How do you rate the skills, training, and experience and your level of achievement within your current job? 1 to 10?

Physical Requirements

What are the physical requirements for this job? Does the job require physical strength or capabilities which are reasonable for now and may not be so reasonable five years from now? Are you sitting all day. No exercise and you are worried about the health consequences? Review all the physical aspects of the job.

Mental and YOU requirements

Are you using your intellectual capabilities? How much or not at all? Does the job suit your talents and your temperament. Remember the discussion on assessing yourself. Is this a rote job which is boring you? Could you, perhaps, change the job to be more interesting and challenging? Again, rate your job on a 1 to 10 scale.

Assess and Rate: Likes, Dislikes, and Neutrals

Now, take an overall assessment of the job? A lot of this 'job assessment' work has been a way of walking through and reviewing all aspects of the job ... not only of the current job, but your expectations for a new job. This process should give you a heads-up and some formative information for when you begin a more detailed decision making process about a career change, transition and new life.

Walk through the details and see how you feel about each aspect of the job assessment and rating. Write down the ratings and your thoughts as you review. Put this into your stack of material for final decision making.

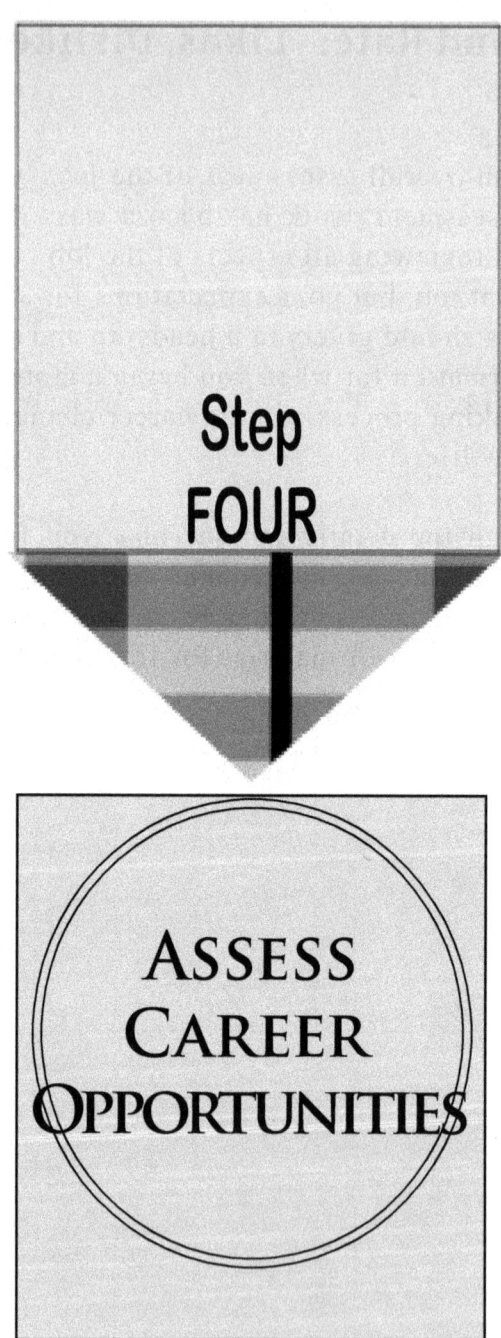

You have assessed your job and you think it may be time for a change. So, what now? Off to the employment pages of the local newspaper? Well, that is certainly part of the next stage of this process. You need to know what is possible for you. What are the career opportunities which you might find interesting .... which play to your strengths, your needs, and your d'ruthers. By this point, you should have spent some time on assessing yourself ... ... i.e. your personality traits, strengths, weaknesses, wants, needs... your own talents, skills, knowledge base. Where do you think you should be looking? You have come to the tentative and preliminary conclusion that the Blue Collar Skilled Trades is your career arena. So, let's talk about how you find out more about the opportunities. What do you need to know ... to make some final decisions about a new career and to act on those decisions.

Making a Career Decision

Making life decisions requires lots of research, analysis and thought. In fact, this is an iterative process. You do the research, analyze what you have found in relationship to the decisions you know you must make. So, keep this in mind while reading these next few chapters. In fact, there are three steps in the process ... research & analysis, decision making, and defining an action plan. You should, however, have much of your research and decision making process accomplished by the time you come to the sit down, make the action plan step.

Choosing your *best fit* skilled trade

Are you looking at Blue Collar Skilled Trades? Have you made a tentative decision? Your starting point should be to make a preliminary choice of the Blue Collar Skilled Trade(s) which fits you --- your capabilities, talents, needs, desires.

There are over 140 skilled trades jobs out there. The number of skilled trades is actually closer to 200 plus. The 140 reflects the ones which are unionized and which usually offer apprenticeships. The unions have made these jobs much better for the workers, but, unfortunately, the gender barrier still exists. Women still have a more difficult time than men in entering the skilled

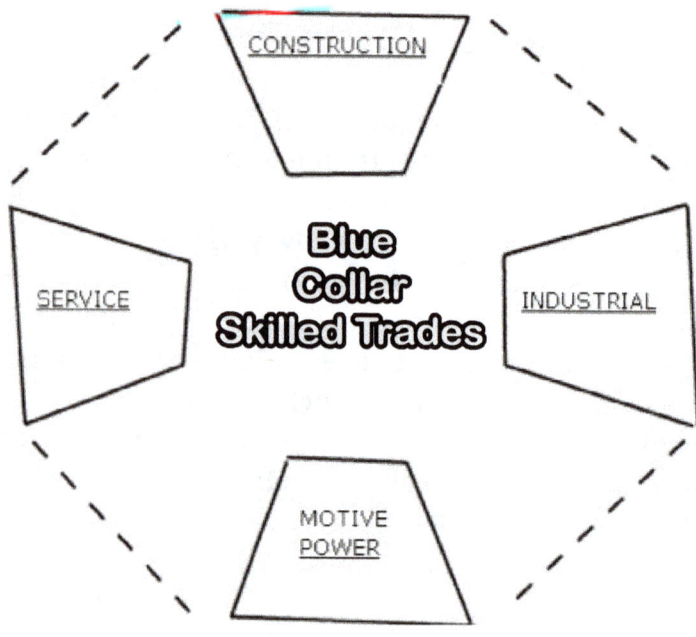

trades -- especially union apprenticeship programs.

Add this topic to your research list -- find out how difficult it is for women to get into the *local* unions. This ABSOLUTELY does not mean that you should not jump into one of these jobs, if you want it. You do need to know whether there is some support group(s) out there to help you --- and just what steps you will need to take to make it happen. (There seem to be a growing and evolving set of support groups and more general help available now which are creating entry into places which were previously closed.)

Your starting research should also include a review of your reading on the various blue collar skilled trades. Maybe you already have some clear idea of what you would like to do -- i.e. you bought a used table saw several years ago and are already building with wood and you think turning this d'ruther and skill set into a vocation would be great. Go to www.bluecollarwoman.com and follow the links to the skilled trades detailed information. Check out links from that website and others listed in the Appendix on support groups (at the end of this book) for lots of other sources for information about carpenters or other trades.

What if ... ... what if you haven't got a clue what blue collar skilled trade you'd d'ruther and what would be best for you? Take a look at the research on Personality Types and Career Choices in the chapter on Assessing Yourself. If you checked out the internet and took some of the tests and found some of the links, follow them up again. Take a look at www.bluecollarwoman.

com for some of the special links which will lead you to those tests and correlations with the personality types to successful career choices. Take some of the tests -- get some free, online, or local career counselor guidance. There is a lot of information out there which expounds on correlations between personality type and career success.

Maureen H told me that she had tested out as an INTJ? She said this didn't surprise her. Said it was actually logical, based on what she knew about herself, so the test seemed OK to her. She gave me the list of jobs which showed up in the personality profile material. She picked out Electrician as something which sounded like she might like it. And... ... guess what, she said last week ---- "It's great. I'm ... like ... a bloomin' great electrician, D. I love it."

(Go to the blue collar woman website and follow the trail to Assessing yourself: personality basics and Choosing your Career.)

Career Research Topics

In order to make decisions about a career change, you will need to explore several different topics:

1. Choosing the right career.
2. Career opportunities.
3. Relevant career information.
4. Schools, Training, Apprenticeships
5. Support for career change and job entry
6. Support for transition into new career.
7. Support for family during transition and career change process.

Those are just some of the topics which you should add to your list to research.

Assess the Career Opportunities

Take a look at what types of careers are available to you. Study the information and associated materials available with our Wheel of Trades both in this book and in the website, www.bluecollarwoman.com. Request some of the manuals on specific trades which may be of interest to you. Continue the research work on the internet. Just put in some key words into your favorite browser (e.g. Google, Bing, Yahoo, etc.) and follow the list of sources. There is a lot of information out there which should help you make some early choices. Here is some of the information from the US Bureau of Labor Statistics as reported in Forbes.com and other online magazines in 2006. They identified the ten best paid blue collar job arenas. This is just a sample of the available information.

Job	Average Annual Pay
Public transit attendant	$ 62,088
Longshore equipment operators	58,198
Brick and stone masons	57,200
Power plant operators	56,472
Locomotive operators	56,347
Aircraft engine mechanics	55,494
Electrical power installers/repairers	55,390
Mining occupations	54,704
Oil well occupations	53,227

> *Here's a few more tidbits re: interesting PAY information. (Go look at the US Department of Labor website for latest data and lots more!)*
>
> Some of the best paying blue collar skilled trades jobs are mechanics, installers and equipment operators -- averaging close to $30 per hour. Some long-haul truck drivers, plumbers and electricians make over $100,000 plus they usually receive excellent benefits.

Choose several trades to research more thoroughly

After you have gone through the materials, take a second look. Choose several of the trades which seem to fit you. Now, review the information and support materials for these trades more carefully. Learn more about the trade - what it takes to get into the field, what are the job activities - i.e. what will you be doing day to day. Does it really pay enough or will the job satisfaction be enough to make the change worthwhile? While you gather information and research these trades, be thinking about the activities, the mental and physical requirements. How do your needs and what you know about yourself fit with these trades?

Dig a little more. Round up the relevant career Information

What do you need to know in order to 1. decide that you REALLY want to DO this job; and 2. How to get in and make it work for you. You will want to know more about what they do, where they work, pay, businesses, personal requirements and capabilities needed. Appendix E includes some sample information for Carpenters. There are a number of websites, including www.bluecollarwoman and a lot of government websites which will detail all this for you ... for each of the specific skilled trades jobs you may find of interest.

Learn as much as you can about it: what it takes to get into the field, what are the job activities - i.e. what will you be doing day to day. pay rates; opportunities.

Make your decision. Do you want to do this and is it worth it? Is the potential job satisfaction enough to make the change. Keep in mind, this involves lots of change for you and your family, hard work to make it happen, costs for training, books, etc.

Develop a plan. This may be one of the most important decisions of your life. It certainly deserves spending some time to think about exactly what you can do to make it happen. The best way to proceed is with a list all those steps you know you must take to change your career. This can be very simple notes of what may seem very obvious to you. However, write them out. For example: 1. Identify what training I need to work in that field as a beginner or apprentice.

The Goldminer's Research Approach

Remember the rules:
Iteration is the great teacher.
Try-fail, try-fail, try-fail, try-succeed, do-succeed.

There is a slightly different variant for research and analysis. It resembles the gold miners shovel and sift approach.
Dig in, lift out some information ('shovel out a bit of dirt'), scratch around in it 'til you find your gold flakes (or maybe a big gold nugget) then go back to dig a little more.

You don't have to finish this in a day. You will learn a lot more and internalize more of the information which is out there waiting for you ... if you take it in small shovel amounts.

Some RESEARCH Tips

Internet Research

The Largest Search Engines are probably

    Google, Yahoo!, Bing

A few more are: MSN Live, Ask, AOL Search

Search Engines index different pages and have different capabilities. You may want to use more than one to find what you are looking for.

Advanced Commands

Use the Advanced commands of the Search Engines. You can save lots of time and almost always find more information which will be helpful.

Search Engine Results (advanced commands are compiled by automated robots that search for and index web pages.)
    These might help for more specifics.
  Google Advanced search help; Google Advanced page.
  Yahoo! Advanced search; Yahoo! shortcuts and More Yahoo! shortcuts
  Bing Advanced (formerly Live search) search options
  Ask Search Tips and Ask Advanced search
  Gigablast Advanced search

Look for:

Web Searching Tips at *Search Engine Watch*
Choose the Best Search Engine for Your...(search) from *Noodle Tools*
Best Search Tools Chart from *InfoPeople*
Pandia All-in-One List for Search Engines and Directories

Do the local research & networking
Apprenticeships, schools, training

There are a number of areas where your research must turn to local sources. You can start with getting local information from the internet. Then you may have to jump on the telephone to round up more direct help. This can be especially true of education and transition programs -- e.g. schools and special tech training; apprenticeships, union and local independent sponsors.

Sometimes making personal contact in the early stages with the right people can both point you in the right direction, highlight some opportunities, and cement some of those opportunities for you. You need to make sure you get as much information up front as possible - especially contacts and timing (e.g. program or school start-end dates.) Getting apprenticeships and union memberships can be extremely important in many of the skilled trades arenas. Money and job availability are often closely tied to these opportunities.

Take the time up front to find out what you need to know and who you need to know to seize any opportunities which might be available. Don't forget the local builder's and women's organizations. There are a number out there and some also have apprenticeships and other programs.

Local Support Programs and Organizations. There are frequently local support organizations ready to help you in your career choosing, transition and job hunting. Find out now what they are and where you can find them. Below are the names of some of these organizations and some ideas about what they can do to help. Call them during this preliminary research phase of your 'NEW LIFE' project. Make contact with some of these people who can help. Get their names, telephone numbers and talk to them about your search and your goals. They may be able to help right now or you may want to recontact them later for support with specific parts of your project.

Some Local Support Organizations
(See Appendix A for more.)

- National Association of Homebuilders
- Chicago Women in Trades;
- New York Women in Trades;
- Tradeswomen, Inc.
- Your local real estate, trade and women's organizations

Find out about local job/career opportunities

Are there lots of jobs available in your town? Have there never been any of these specific types of jobs locally available? For instance, if you have decided that you want to be a steam fitter and you live in Florida or Arizona -- you see the possible issues here? Also, during some down times in the economy, many of the jobs related to construction become scarce. That is a normal pattern. You should find out what these patterns appear to be for your local communities. Can you survive the downturns? And, if so, how would you handle them?

This is a perenial problem for those in the construction industry and many are struggling during a particularly somber recession right now. Talk to some of the local contractors. What do they think about long term potential in your area?

Training Requirements, Costs and Availability

The formal training for a skilled trade can take two to five years and includes both classroom and hands on work. However, you should be earning money within a year or so or earlier, depending on the type of training you choose. There are community colleges and technical schools, as well as, trade programs at the local high schools. The most highly recommended approach is an apprenticeship in your selected trade with the associated union or an independent group.

The costs will range from zero to thousands of dollars, depending on your choices and the availability of the special programs. The private, for profit, technical schools are the most costly to you and they may offer to help with loans. *About going into debt for school ....* If at all possible, don't do it. That is no way to begin a new career. You will have enough stress without this added financial burden. Review the full list of support groups and training and apprenticeship opportunities in your area. Talk directly with the sponsors and counselors.

How much training you will need, of course, depends on where you start. Have you had classes in high school, been exposed to or even worked in the field at some time?

Specific Support for Apprenticeship and Job Entry

As you talk with local groups - have your list of questions available. One set of those questions should relate to the availability of apprenticeships. Union offices, technical schools, and local/national independent construction and building associations are good sources. They will be able to tell you what is available -- what the requirements are -- and how competitive these positions are. In many cases, there are organizations which will provide preliminary training and coaching for the actual apprenticeship application and tests. You may need some remedial classes in math and English or other topics. They will be able to tell you what you will face and give you a better idea how to give yourself the best chance of success.

At the same time, in the same research/discovery meetings with these local contacts, check out what they think about job opportunities. You may even be talking with someone who can make hiring decisions for great starting jobs. Make sure you have a complete 'research question' list which will allow you to get details about specific jobs, companies, who to talk with, what is needed (job requirements), any specific schools which are considered good to excellent. These companies may hire from specific schools and refuse other graduates based on their hiring experience. Find out.

Again, be prepared with a detailed list of subjects and questions and essentially the information you will need to select schools, find out about apprenticeships and get a job.

Entrepreneur?

Decide whether you would prefer to work for someone else or start your own business. Take a look at the support materials on running a business. Also, consider the requirements for starting and running your own business - financial, time, stress, work effort. You may want to do it. But you may need to wait ... to plan that as a future goal. Future does not have to mean never.

Are you a hands-on person or would you rather run your own business? Want to own a contracting business and tackle all the logistics of running a business? or do you want to carry tools around and wire a house or a commercial building? Very big difference in those jobs.

Face the Realities

Getting apprenticeships and union memberships can be extremely important in many of the skilled trades arenas. Money and job availability are frequently tied to union membership. It is still difficult for women to get past the roadblocks and harassment factors in these 'non-traditional' jobs. The Civil Rights Act of 1964 made it illegal to discriminate against employees on the basis of race, color, religion, and sex. This law officially gave women the legal access to the skilled trades jobs which had effectively been almost completely closed to them. Unfortunately, in many cases, these unionized groups are still effectively mostly male. My research has shown that strong unionized groups, like large city

Fire Departments, still may have only token female membership. One source listed less than 40 females out of 11,000 in a major American city; and that is not unusual.

In 1978, the Department of Labor set affirmative action goals for hiring women on publicly financed construction sites. Great idea. However, today, over thirty years later, women still make up less than 3 percent of the skilled trades workers (4 to 6 million.)

So ... in planning for, training for and finding a job, you need to face the realities. AND, you need to ensure that you are ready with an action plan to make it happen for you - despite those realities.

Reality number one that any women must face in making the decision to change careers, to move into a skilled trades job is this: There is a very real systematic exclusion of females and other minority workers from many union locals, apprenticeship programs and unionized work projects.

Reality number two is that there is a very real barrier of harassment in many of those jobs which have been traditionally held exclusively by males. Women have made some gains since the Civil Rights Act, but the problems of harassment, lack of union representation, isolation and sexist attitudes are still pervasive and present major obstacles to women entering and staying in non-traditional jobs.

Reality number three These are high paying jobs with excellent benefits. These are jobs which you can do and which may very well be much better for you than the one you have now.

Reality number four You may need to fight for the opportunity. You may have to ignore slurs, bad language, and entry hurdles.

Reality number five You must face the realities, plan on them, and deal with them. If you decide that the job is what you want and need, you may have to fight for it.

Go for it.

Make it Happen.

DO IT.

BLUE COLLAR WOMAN®
Yes We Can!

5. Decide and Plan

Make Decisions for a New Life

Plan Your Course:
Plan, Review, Consult

Step FIVE

Make Decisions for a New Life

> **Can you commit NOW to improving your life?**

Foundation for Happiness:

Something to do that you love

Someone to love

Somthing to look forward to

Good Health

Finances sufficient to your needs

also ...
Happiness requires hope, commitment and a passionate involvement.

Will making a career change lead you to a fuller life, more joyful living, and work to do that you can do with passion? Some of us luck into one or even all five of the 'happiness' basics. Some of us have to work harder at it. We have to make our own happiness. The two foundations: the 'something to do that you love' and the 'financial stability' are for most people tied to a job ... a career. Unless you are wealthy (and therefore most likely not reading this book) then decisions about your career will impact at least two of these happiness basics, i.e. finding something to do that you can be passionate about and having the financial resources to lead the life which you want. A job change may be your next step in achieving some of your life goals.

Deciding on a New Career

Deciding that you want a new career translates into not one decision, but essentially into a cascading set of decisions. You need to know what those questions and decisions are; what is involved and the timing for each. You should make the decisions from a base of knowledge and strength. That means you will anticipate each, research each, make some preliminary decisions, then analyze, meditate and role play the results and projected changes to your life. This is a process ... research, decision making and action planning. The process is iterative -- research, analysis, tentative decisions, and planning; then review and reprocess and firm up plans. Then, step through it again.

Some of the immediate, first level decisions which you may face now are:

1. Do you *want* a different job? A new career?
2. What do you want your new job to be? Do you want a hands-on job or do you want to be an entrepreneur? In either case, what job should it be? *or* perhaps: What aspect of entrepreneurship? For example, do you want to be a construction contractor or a marketing expert?
3. If you go for a skilled trades job, you will need to ensure that the job you choose is one that is suitable for you and your family. In addition, and critical to the decision process, recognize that minimum wage, unskilled or barely skilled is not what you need or want. Make sure the job you select includes skills which are well regarded and marketable both now and in the long term.

4. Do you want a new life: finances, environment, life patterns? Many times, the decisions for one and two will give you the answers, at least partially, the decisions about the new life.
5. Can you change your job and career right now? If not, can you project a time frame? Do you want to wait? This decision has to do with the practical aspects of transitioning into a new career? Money, family responsibilities, partner and family support or lack of support, and more.
6. Who are you? Do you have the drive, the guts, the passion to make a plan and push through all obstacles?

These are just some of the decisions and questions on which you need to focus up front.

Go or No Go?

Here are some questions to begin the process -- making a decision to change your career and your life. Self analysis and life analysis comes first. You need to answer some of the big questions for yourself.

> D'ruthers, Yearnings,
> Passions & Values
> Talents, Skills and Knowledge

You should carefully consider what your thoughts are on such questions as:

- Where to Work? Best Work Environment
- Entrepreneur? or work for someone else, at least for now?

You will need to carefully analyze and understand the logistics of your life. (Maybe you already are completely aware of these.) Your responsibilities, you daily pattern of living and many other life factors will determine just how easy or difficult major life changes will be for you. You can do it, but you need to understand what that will mean for your life. What will a career change and a disruptive transition mean for your practical daily living? Can you manage the new personal stress, the financial requirements, and the family upheaval? You may really want a change. BUT ... can you manage it NOW? Do you need to give yourself a bit longer to plan for the change and to prepare?

Would the timing be better in the fall when the kids are in school or is there some other life balancing act you need to consider? Think about the timing. Be realistic and practical. It may not be lack of 'drive' or 'guts' which leads to a NO decision. It may be a reasoned, practical response to current reality.

So... ... you need to think about not only what you want to do, you need to consider the decisions which need to be made in transitioning to the new career. For example, you will need to consider:

> Your personal transition: training, education, apprenticeship, job entry; as well as,
> Your family transition - kids, spouses, friends, support network.

What's your gut say?

Answer the questions with your gut, your heart, and your common sense.

- Do you want a change?
- Do you know what you want to do?
- If not, how will you make a decision?
- How strongly do you want a change?
- Do you envision changing your life to change your life? By this I mean: *Do you understand that your daily pattern of living must change in order to accomplish your goals.* Can you do that? Do you want this new career and new life enough to handle a rough transition period?
- Can you 'make it happen' --- i.e. money wise, time wise, kid wise, family wise --- for however long it takes? How long is that?
  - Is the best job in terms of what you'd **d'ruther** the best job in terms of what will work for you and your family?
  and ... ...
  Should this even be a consideration?
- How long will the transition take and can you support your positive attitude and drive, as well as, your family's needs for that long?
- Do you have the support of your family? your friends? your life partner?
- How will you support you and your family if you leave your current job? Can you keep your current job and transition while working? (VERY tough --- think carefully about this.)
- Do you absolutely know what you want to do? or do you need to explore further with a professional? or

more self assessment and career research?
- If you choose one career ... can you turn it into something else if you decide it is not exactly what you want? You vs jobs/careers/opportunities?
- What are the local possibilities -- training, apprenticeships, jobs now, career future?
- Could you move, if necessary?
- How will you take care of your children, i.e. get your daily living stuff done?

Skilled Trade - Which One?

<u>Next level of the Decision Process:</u> Research, analyze and dig a little deeper. Learn more about the blue collar skilled trades and jobs. Take a look at what types of careers are available to you. Study the information and associated materials available with the Blue Collar Woman® Wheel of Trades (www.bluecollarwoman.com). Follow up on the additional sources identified in the appendices. There is a tremendous amount of information available on the internet.

Choose a trade that works for you. Review the information and support materials. Think about what kinds of activities would make you most content. Compare your own personal needs and goals with those which are noted for the specific skilled trade and/or job or business. That includes time, stress, finances, and current family obligations. In addition, and perhaps more important than anything else --- how strong is your desire --- what are your motivations and how much are they eating into your 'gut'.

One, Two, Three:
Make some preliminary decisions

You started the decision process only because you already had at least a 'gut' feel that you want to change your career. Now, you have done some research and reviewed and responded to the questions for yourself about the changes, the responsibilities and the opportunities. So, do you still think you want a change? Do you think you can make change happen? Do you understand a little better what will be involved? Give yourself at least a day or so to integrate your research, your preliminary thoughts, the questions and answers about your life and circumstances. Then answer the questions again. Think again about what you want from life.

Research, Analyze, Meditate, Role play

Take the time now to do more research into the new career, the local opportunities, the support factors involved with transition, both family wise and career wise. Give yourself at least a day or so to integrate your research, your preliminary thoughts, the questions and answers about your life and circumstances. Then answer the questions again. Think again about what you want from life. Think again about who you are, what your current life is like, your responsibilities and goals. Do you have the desire, the passion and the positive attitude and driving power to make the necessary changes?

Role play means to mentally place yourself in the circumstances of a new set of stresses and life activities of your new, transitional life. You will be living a whole new life --- perhaps finding someone else to pick up the kids, going off to school yourself, practicing a new set of skills, making sure your partner fixes dinner and runs more errands. Experience and act out for yourself what those changes will mean in terms of every day life and trials and perhaps heartache and headaches.

This is not a time for snap decisions. It is great to dream about a new life. It will be a tough job to build that new life. Give yourself at least a week (or longer) to stew and boil and ponder about the ingredients for your new life.

Discuss all the aspects of the process with yourself. Understand and integrate them for yourself. Now, pick some trusted friends and family and discuss with them what you are going through. (This is your support network - whoever you feel comfortable talking with, actually). Get their feedback and listen to it carefully.

One of the major mistakes people make, I think, is to ask for advice, then forget to listen to it. You have chosen to talk with these people because they know you and presumably care for you.
                   Listen!

Make sure you find out why they think what they do. Why are they saying -- yes, do this, or no, do that. (Cannot's should be carefully considered and, hopefully, overcome.) Get details. Make sure you understand the rationale for their yes or no advice. Do they think you have too many responsibilities? Do they think you cannot do the new job? Why? and why do you agree or disagree with them.
               This is **your** decision!

Get help with it, if you can. But remember: **you** are the person who is ultimately responsible for making any change work for you.

Decide. (with wiggle room)

When you feel that you have fully comprehended and integrated all the factors, then make your tentative decision. If that decision is STILL to go with life change ---- if that decision is to make a career change -- then great! Go ahead.

Keep in mind and believe this:
   It is definitely OK to decide to wait or not to make that change.
            This is *your* life.

Hands-on or Entrepreneur?

This is a decision which can be decided in steps. You may elect to go with a hands-on skilled trade -- then, later, you may wish to turn that into a business for yourself. In fact, many people find this is the best route. Unless you have a driving personal need or other specific reasons to start out as an entrepreneur, you will most likely elect to go hands-on for now. A reason specific to your circumstances may be a family business or some personal business management skills. Consider all these aspects of you and your life. Making the life and career changes MAY be easier as a step process --- hands-on skill development/salaried job then going for your own business. There is a lot of additional work in starting and running a business. If you are being drawn to starting a business of your own, then take a look at the support materials on running a business (on the internet - including www.bluecollarwoman.com) Consider the requirements for starting and running your own business. Make the decision based on your own needs, circumstances and d'ruthers.

Decide on Training, Apprenticeships and Transition

Decisions about your training for the selected skilled trades job are especially important. They must, of course, be based on what is available to you, in your chosen living/local area. If you can find the support and get yourself into an apprenticeship program with either a union or an independent organization, do that. It is your best alternative.

If not, then you will most likely have to get some training through local technical schools or community colleges. The community college is your best choice here. If they have the skills training that you need, then the costs will be more acceptable. Some of the technical schools are excellent and may have a good reputation in your area. In your research, be sure to follow up on their job referrals, placement/success rate, and reputation among employers. You must also consider whether you can afford any higher costs and explore carefully your alternatives.

In your research, find out about local support organizations. Go with an apprenticeship program if at all possible.

Your research into the schools and technical training options are particularly important in making these decisions and plans. You may need training prior to the apprenticeship program, but most likely that will not be a must. Again, if there is a community college nearby which offers the training you need, that may be your best bet. The costs will be lower; the program focused on general as well as local needs. The decision about training should include several considerations:

- Local Availability
- Costs
- Appropriateness
- Comprehensiveness
- Meets requirements of (recommended by) local hiring managers

Career Entry Decisions

Apprenticeship programs offer easy transition into the career of your choice. Other choices of schools and training will influence the career opportunities which will be available to you. That means, of course, that the research and decisions you have made during this entire process will directly impact the success of your career.

Do the research into opportunities, school and training reputations, and requirements BEFORE you walk too far down the career change path. Do NOT be one of those who are led into enormous debt and poor skills by fraudulent or near fraudulent advertising and marketing ploys. Look behind the ads and the promises. Do not sign or commit without seeking objective, outside advice.

Make the Decisions?

So --- make a decision to change. How do you make that decision?

1. Do you want to make a change?
2. How badly do you want it?

3. What do you think you want to do?
4. Do you have the capabilities to do what you want?
5. Do you have or can you get the skills?
6. Is it possible within the framework of your life right now-- family, finances, support systems?
7. Can you make it work at another time -- better?
8. Can you make it work now --- will you have the drive and determination to struggle through the transition process? Do you have the support systems --- i.e. people who will listen to you kvetch and will also care enough to go get your kids from school --- lots?
9. Can you get assistance for school and training ---- this should be part of your research --- there are more and more support and assistance groups for women who need help.
10. If your answer to all these is 'YES I CAN', you still have to understand what is involved and be willing to say 'YES I WILL'.

Go
for
IT!

Why a special section just on planning. It is so obvious what needs to be done. You have already gone through a lot of research and decision making and the thought process involved in making these career decisions. You have seen what training is necessary and probably already know how you are going to make that happen. So, why do you need a special stage in this career change business just for planning. Just get started, for crying out loud. You know what to do now. Right?

NO! **A lot is riding on this.** AND You need to finalize such topics as ... setting out in some detail exactly what are your goals, interim and final. A plan should be detailed. Just the process of coming up with the *detailed* list of action items should trigger some 'Oh, of course. I need to add/do that' thoughts.

So let's walk through the planning process and decide exactly what you need to include.

Set Goals

There are several sets of goals to be concerned with: final and transition achievement goals and those goals which are necessary because they are tied to the final and transition achievement goals. For example, you may have to study and pass a test as part of the process of going for an apprenticeship or becoming certified. The final or achievement goals which you have already decided on should now be defined again and actually written down -- like all your plan. What are those achievement goals? Do you want to become a journey level electrician and make that happen in five years? Do you want to be earning a rate of pay which is 35% greater than now within two years and a final rate at the recognized journey level by the end of five years? Do you want to go to a specific school, take some specific training? Sign up and apply for apprenticeship with a local independent group or the local union?   Define each of the goals. Write each one down on paper.

Define Action Steps

Make sure you know and clearly describe each step which is involved in achieving those goals. Write them down. Tie times and finances and requirements. If you need to take a prep course prior to going for an apprenticeship test, then figure out which one and make sure you include all the specifics, including time, contacts, costs. Include your sign up information for any transition step. For example, is there a technical course you want to take and have been convinced will help you with a job in your field.   Where, how much, timing, sign up information, prerequisites? Have you checked out any apprenticeships or relationships with business which are part of the technical school/community college curriculum?   Follow up and add the research, contacts, and follow through to your list of action steps. Essentially, you need to walk through every step, every facet of your career change, list it in your plans, find out everything you can about that step -- and describe it in detail. You will be expanding your knowledge of the path to your successful transition into your new career.

Describe Alternative/Fallback Plans

What will you do if you do not pass the apprenticeship test which you have picked out? What will you do if your mother cannot take care of the children while you are in school in August? How about getting into the technical school or community college. Do you have the course credits required to even start the program?

Ask yourself these types of questions about every step of your action plan. Set up some contingency plans for alternative routes. Also, what kind of emergencies could occur? Do you know what you can do in those cases?

Color in the Details

Making your plan involves sitting down with paper and pen. Make your first draft as a list of items -- actions, tasks, activities ... all those things which come to mind and which have come up during research and decision making steps. Next -- after the basic list -- start coloring in the details. If you know, for example, that you want to attend an eighteen month program at the local community college, write that down. Now list and describe all the details you already know about that action/activity. For example, list the logistics of getting there on a daily basis, a babysitter (if required) and, of course, all the incidentals about the classes, timing, books, and more.

Set Time Lines

Add the times for each of the interim steps. You should know by now school dates, test dates, and more.

If you haven't already laid out your major time line, do it now. This includes start and end dates from now through achieving your major end goal -- e.g. becoming a journey level electrician and having a fantastic job. Then add on the times for each of the interim achievements - or progress steps. Then add more details and times - until you can see in your timeline all those activities and tasks which you will be living over the next few years.

Define relationships to research, decisions and the decision process

You did a lot of research and went through an extensive decision process to get to this paper planning process. Think through that research and those decisions. Think about the networking which you have done. Be sure to add all the people and contacts and possibilities to your activities and tasks. Follow up where necessary. Make sure that you cover any potential support and jobs possibilities in your planning. You may need to follow up on more of these. Keep the information available to you and remember to go back and use it in case an emergency/fallback position is necessary. Also, don't forget to add a thank you list for yourself. And ...
    be sure that you remember to go personally and thank each person who helped along the way.

Define requirements for success

Define the requirements for success for each action step and for the overall and interim goals you have written into your plan. Be specific. If there are people involved and you know you will need their help during the process, make sure to include what has to be done to enlist that help.

Review your plan

A simple step: effective and sometimes just seemingly too much trouble. Review everything on your plan. Read and integrate each action/activity/task again. Understand what you will be doing, when, and who will be involved. Think it through again. Make sure it works for you.

Consult with and get sign off from your support and interface network

Call your support group together, or get to them separately. Review the plan with them. Make sure that they agree what you have laid out is doable. You want two things here. You want separate opinions and review of your thoughts. One: Do they agree that it seems a good, viable plan? And, two: you want to make sure that IF they are to be involved in any capacity, that they understand their role, agree to the role and say **'yes'** - go ahead. I'm with you on this.

BLUE COLLAR WOMAN®
Yes We Can!

6. Do It ... ... Live It

Make it Happen: Schools, Training, Transition

Make it Happen: Get A Job

Make it Happen: Live Your New Life

ow is the **Make it Happen** time. By Now .... you have researched and analyzed:
YOU... ...
YOUR LIFE... ...
YOUR JOB... ...

You have studied the skilled trades jobs ... .. and taken a preliminary look at which skilled trades job is for you. You have researched and reviewed local opportunities, apprenticeship programs and schools. Timing of the schools, programs and tests have been integrated into your review and planning lists.

NOW --- you need to begin your route to success. Fill out the forms, apply for the programs, enroll in school, take the preliminary tests, get your support programs and make sure your finances are in place. And... ... get started in a school, apprenticeship program, on-the-job training or a self apprenticeship job.

In this chapter, we will review each of those programs and activities and describe some of them in more detail. This is the time to make sure you have covered all the bases. Get on with the transition into your new career.

Career Transition --- Schools and Training

There are a number of routes to a successful new career in the skilled trades arena. Most of these involve some form of formal in-class instruction, on the job training, and preliminary job hands-on (OK, that sounds like more 'on the job' training to me, too.) So what are the routes you can take to transition into your new career?

Best Routes, Good Routes and *"I Don't think so"* back roads

I. Best Route
Sponsored Apprenticeship Program

The best program, the very best route, into the skilled trades is an Apprenticeship Program which is regulated by federal and state based agencies, regulations and laws. The best of these programs are based on laws and federal and state regulations which offer you a guaranteed route through the career change. The apprenticeships may be sponsored by unions, independent associations or stand alone businesses. Unions are probably the most likely sponsors, but there are builders associations and other groups out there. With a sponsored apprenticeship you get tuition free, formal, structured education and on the job hands-on skilled trades learning, i.e. classroom instruction combined with on-the-job training. You get paid while you learn and when you finish the program you will have recognized credentials which open the job market for you across the country (and the world). The apprenticeship programs may take from 3 to 6 years or so. The average seems to be about 5 years. However, during those years, you may count on a good wage -- a wage which is based on a percentage of that paid to a journeyman/journeywoman and which is known up front and increases at a set and contracted, preset rate over the time of the apprenticeship. The program is set up to give you all the in class and on the job training you need, as well as, the preparation for and the opportunities to take the necessary qualifying tests. For some of the programs you will need special certifications. For example, there is almost always a certification requirement to work as an electrician. When you finish a specialized apprenticeship program, you will be an experienced worker with recognized credentials in your selected skilled trade. AND, you will have been paid to make the journey.

Sponsored Apprenticeship:

> This is the best way. Research, explore, and find the one for you. If you can get into an apprenticeship program -- go for it!

II. Good Route
Community College plus Hands-on

You can also sign up with your local community college for a program in your selected trade and find a training program or on-the-job training program with a local employer. The community colleges are publicly funded or at least subsidized. The community colleges do not necessarily focus on skilled trades training. However, many have excellent programs. These community colleges are also frequently the foundation and a good connection place for the more formal, structured federal/state recognized apprenticeship programs. Actually, this career transition route may be somewhat more informal than a standard apprenticeship entry -- but it can still give you some excellent training and career entry. It can also provide some connection to local employers, since local employers most often look for their hires from local schools. You can aim for an associate's degree or other certification and perhaps, even, customize your own in-class education and on the job training.

The major drawbacks are that you do not have the 'guarantees' of skills acquisition and transferability. You do not have a guaranteed wage scale and you will most likely have to pay for the community college class room program. However, this **is** an excellent transition route into the skilled trades. The community college contacts and support can be invaluable in introductions and support for your new career.

The Community Colleges and other local community and state sponsored training and education institutes are a good alternative way to get into your chosen new field.

Consider ... ... Explore this option and during the research steps, network. Look for contact information and support from the college counselors. They may be able to help slot you into some of the apprenticeship programs which they most likely have worked out with local employers, unions and state apprenticeship councils. Never give up on contacts and networking to get you into the program you need and one which is best suited to you.

IIIa.   Another Good Route.
Self Apprenticeship

This route is pretty basic:
  Go find someone you like in the business and convince them to let you work for them and learn the business from them.

You may have to offer to work for nothing for awhile... or just a low ball wage. Your negotiating and presentations skills here are critical, of course. If you can convince someone of your value and that they will benefit in the long term from such an arrangement, great. Honor your word and their trust. Just jump in, hang on, learn all that you can, when you can, as it is offered. Make it your job to learn as fast as possible. At the same time, register and go on to a community college/ tech course. In most cases you can find classes which you can layer around your job times. Make sure your boss knows and approves of what you are doing.

This is a good way to jump in and get a fast orientation to your new career ---- if you can find someone you like to work with and who will work with you.

IIIb. Alternative.
Self Apprenticeship/Family Business

There is, of course, the self apprenticeship alternative which involves having family or close friends in a business. You can tap into this ready made opportunity to get in the business. If you have this alternative available to you -- then you may have already selected your route and are looking only for some formal in-class training. If you have a pass into a business you can be comfortable with and learn to love --- use it. Take advantage of whatever fast steps are available to you.

IV. Good, so-so, or 'don't go there' Route

Technical Colleges and Technical Schools
(Research very carefully before signing anything.)

There are some excellent technical schools, both *for profit* and also some which are essentially supported by local school boards and other government systems. Any warnings here are definitely not for the technical schools which are locally and state sponsored. Many of these have just transitioned themselves from the 'community college' mode. They may have changed their name and focus to specialized programs. These can be a great way to get your training, your education and move into your chosen field. You can get the same types of connections and support from the counselors here as from the community colleges. You may have one near you.

You need to be wary of some of the other *for-profit* technical schools out there. The quality of the training may be good or not so good. You can recognize the ones to be wary of in a number of ways. Their websites are most often very professional, polished and essentially empty of information. There is nothing about tuition and no training details on these websites. For every click you make, the response is a form you must fill in with detailed information about yourself. When you call the '800' number which is usually the only other contact information, you are told that they cannot give you tuition rates or program information. You must fill in the form and a *representative* will contact you. I made numerous calls to several of the schools and got absolutely nothing. No way would they give any information about tuition or the program online or by telephone. Contrast this with the straight forward approach of the community colleges and other technical schools. For example: Here is the fee structure of the North GA Technology School from their website on June/2011.

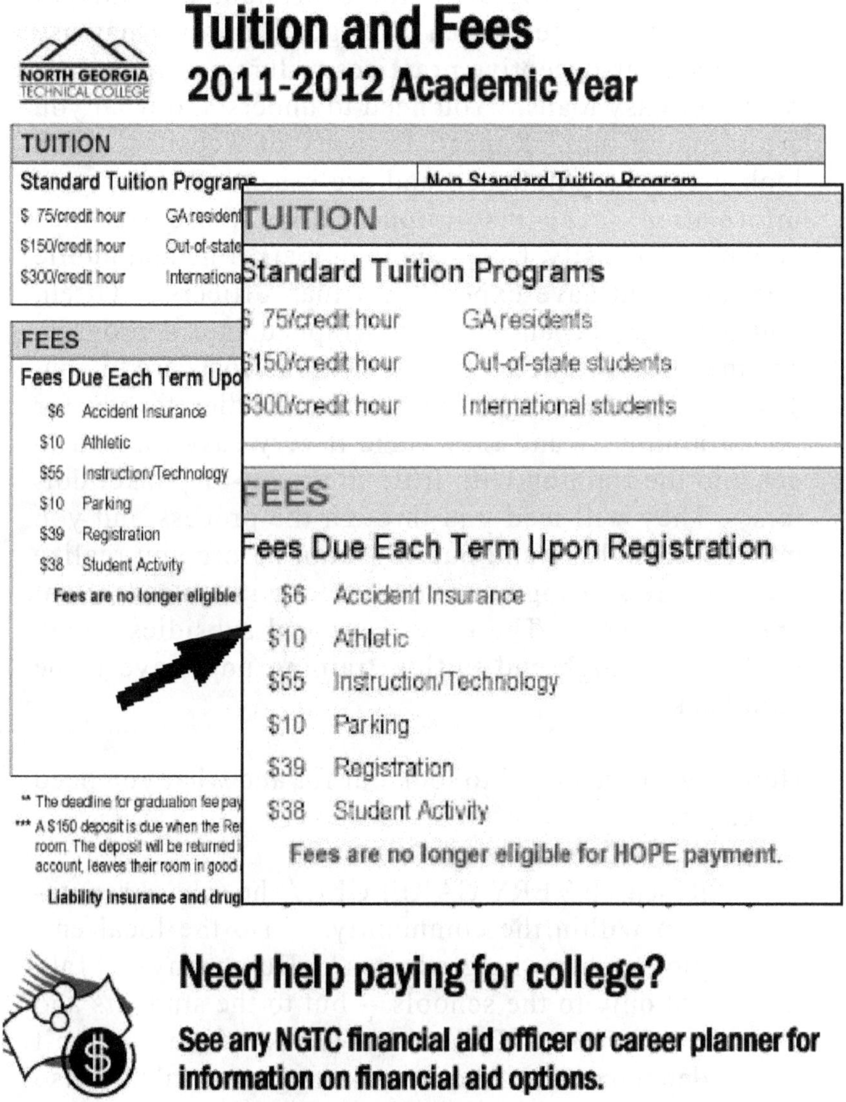

Tuition and Fees
2011-2012 Academic Year

TUITION

Standard Tuition Programs

$75/credit hour	GA residents
$150/credit hour	Out-of-state students
$300/credit hour	International students

FEES

Fees Due Each Term Upon Registration

- $6 Accident Insurance
- $10 Athletic
- $55 Instruction/Technology
- $10 Parking
- $39 Registration
- $38 Student Activity

Fees are no longer eligible for HOPE payment.

Need help paying for college?
See any NGTC financial aid officer or career planner for information on financial aid options.

With some of the 'for profit' schools, you may end up paying high tuition rates for training that may be good or only mediocre. Local employers may or may not find graduates from these schools acceptable. You need to do a lot of research before you commit to one of these schools. The major issue for you is that you could walk away from the program with exorbitant amounts of debt. Even the ones which offer good training may use the same near-deceptive practices to lure you in and arrange for easy loans. You need to understand what you are stepping into. Repeat: Be wary of websites which look great, very polished and are essentially empty of information. The institutions behind these websites may be very costly, have excellent marketing and public relations, and have experienced loan officers. Often, you are enrolled and rapidly wrapped into a program and may not really understand what the costs are to you. They know how to get loans and subsidies to pay for your training --- and they make it very easy for you to get into the training with little to no out-of-pocket dollars. They will lead you through the process and you may be actually in and out of school before you realize that you are starting your new career with an exorbitant amount of debt. The easy loans and subsidies which paid for the high-end tuition training now have to be paid back.

Here is what you need to look out for and what you need to research:

- Research VERY CAREFULLY the school reputation within the community. Do the local employers hire the graduates? How many? Talk not only to the schools -- but to the students and employers. Call them. Go see them. Don't depend on the school marketing materials. (Also

-- it can't hurt to remember -- at the same time you are doing the research, you are meeting and making contacts -- for both jobs and maybe even transition support. Never can tell who you might meet and who might be able to help you now and later.) What do local employers think about the school and the training? Talk to some of the employers you may be interested in joining. Don't take the *representative's* word or some brochure or other marketing material.
- How do the tuition rates compare with community colleges? You can expect them to be higher ... but how much higher?
  - Are they selling you on funding school with loans? Can you understand the process ... and the amounts, as well as, the loan rates involved? What will you owe when you finish the program? How will you repay these loans?

<u>Worth Repeating</u>

These schools usually have well trained funding people -- who know exactly how to get money for your tuition in the form of loans. They make it EASY and FAST. They have the contacts, all the forms, and you mostly talk and sign. These institutions are usually the most expensive route on your list of career transition options. VERY Expensive! As noted before, they also will make it very easy for you to get tuition/financial aid. They are set up to do that. BUT, this can be a deadly trap!!!!! You will have to repay those expenses, in full. AND...

Just a little aside here: Currently, I think, these school loans are not even wiped away by personal bankruptcy. These debts can haunt you for a long time. So get some outside, objective advice ... before you sign anything.

Go for the training and hands-on experience you need to get the job..... whatever that means for you and your chosen career. If you can make it happen, get into an apprenticeship program. If not, go for any combination of skilled trades on-the-job training and in-class instruction which will land you the job. Make the contacts, get some counseling, research what is out there for you and talk to the people who know.

Networking is critical. Call, visit, and talk to people who might be able to help.

More about Apprenticeships and Technical Schools in Appendix D

If your job and training route was through an apprenticeship, fantastic! You are already there. Congratulations. You have your first job and the credentials for a long term career in your chosen field.

Finding a Job

Getting a job in a blue collar skilled trade these days is not so different than 'getting a job' period. You need to know what to do, who to see, and you need to have an action plan. Research and planning for getting a job are just as critical as research and planning to train for a job. Unfortunately, great training and graduation from a technical school does not magically materialize a job for you. You will not necessarily walk automatically from your skilled trades training into a great job. There can be a lot of work involved in finding the right job. Before you even begin your training, you should select some prospective employers, companies for whom you might like to work. It would be a good idea to make some contact with those employers early in the training process. The schools can help you there, too. Use them and their contacts before, during and after your formal training.

Finding a job is, itself, a job ... and a major project. Now is the time to bear down and grind out the power steps which will lead you to getting a great job.

How long will it take?

If you were very lucky and went into an apprenticeship program, you are already there. You have a job and you have a certification in your field which will get you a job anywhere.

On the other hand. If not --- it can take anywhere from one day, two days, two months, six months. However, with the training you now have and the contacts you have made during that training and transition time, you should be able to get a job in the shorter period of time. If it takes longer, then get some help from local support groups and counselors. You should consider doing that up front anyway, unless a job appears within the first day or two of searching. (Go talk with your community college business interface or other support group contacts -- ask them for some good, common sense advice. Ask them for job contacts.) If it is taking too long, then there may also be some issues in the whole economy or in your local economy which must be taken into account. If it is a local problem, you may need to, at least, consider relocating.

Action Steps in Finding a Great Job

Some of the same steps in the process of selecting and training for a career are critical in getting a job.

- Run on your own internal generator. You need to provide your own power, passion, determination.

- Decide and clearly describe: What are you looking for in a job?

- Develop your strategy and approach to finding a job.

- Enlist your support network.

- Research the job prospects and employers.

- Network; find and use the hidden market; and call on support groups.

- Create power resumes, letters and applications.

- Interview with professionalism, enthusiasm and likeability.

- Negotiate for the best possible wages and benefits.

YES WE CAN.
Power, Passion, Determination

You need to know yourself and what motivates you. Can you throw yourself into this with the same passion we talked about before? YES WE CAN is not just a slogan -- it reflects the power, the determination, the passion to make it happen for YOU. So what does that mean? You need to be organized, have a great resume, a great customized cover letter for *each* employer, make your list of employers, get your contacts, call/call/call, meet with job services, job placement people and know what the local job boards and counseling services are and use them.

What do you want from the Job

Walk through your goals again. Define what you want from a job. Now that you have completed the training, you should have a much more clear idea about what a job can offer you. You have trained for the job. Is this job on which you are focusing now -- is this the job you trained for? Do the skills, the activities and tasks, as you see them in this job, match what you can do with the training you have so far? Did the schools and training prepare you for this job? What exactly *should* you be looking for in terms of skills, activities, tasks in the job?

What hours, location, people skills and trade skills do you expect to see in the job? What stated goals from the employer do you expect?

Develop your strategy for finding a job

What are the ways to find a job?

> Read and respond to the classified ads; employment agencies; submit applications to places you think might be hiring or where you might like to work; research online job banks. Word of mouth; networking; employment agencies; informal 'walk-ins'. Support organizations. Network - network - network. Family and Friends and casual acquaintances - referrals and jobs information.

Those first four ways, although you need to follow through with them, may be the least productive. Most jobs are found through the 'hidden job market'. That hidden job market includes those jobs which are not listed anywhere - but the word is out from those who work at the location, their family, friends, and general gossip. In the white collar management fields, this may have been called the 'old boys' network'. But that was just because their family and friends were the 'old boys'. The key here is that all your family and friends and acquaintances, including school and special support groups, should be considered your network. Follow-up now on all the preliminary work from the school, training and transition processes: Referrals from community colleges and technical schools; support organizations; preliminary contacts with companies and job prospects. Make those contacts pay off now.

The best way to find a job is a combination of all these strategies and approaches. The most critical is this: Contacts, contacts, contacts. That must be first on your list. Talk to everyone you know about jobs and job prospects. Listen to the responses. Follow-up on any glimmers of ideas or prospects. You should, of course, also do the other research, e.g. internet, classified, jobs boards, to find out what the opportunities and job potential sites are in your local area. Then, make direct contact. However, those contacts you have made along the way aren't always breaking down your door with jobs. You may need to keep your hand in with the classified ads, job services, and job boards. Use all the resources and contacts and methods available to you.

Enlist your Support Network

Many of the same people who have supported you through the job training and transition process will be there to help you with the job hunting. What are their special talents? Maybe your children's caretaker (your mother?) is really good with words and can help with a resume? Perhaps the Saturday lunch group has contacts for jobs?

The point here is to ensure that you talk with and enlist the assistance of everyone you know in your job hunting experience. Get the word out through them. Listen carefully. Follow up on any feedback they give you.

Research the job prospects and employers

The research you need to do on available jobs, prospective companies and best employers in the local area should have been started long ago in the early parts of your career change process. Internet research, local contacts including school business connections and interfaces, support groups, local skilled trades associations and local, statewide and international women's support and other organizations. You should also find out what are the companies in the local area who may hire and, in particular, which may hire the skills you have been working to acquire.

Work your strategy:
network, network, network

Your strategy should include all those job *search and find* techniques mentioned previously -- e.g. classified ads, job boards, internet classified and search, and networking. You must maintain your patience and determination. Keep plugging at all the sources.

Create Power Resumes, letters, applications

Resumes? Do you need one?

ABSOLUTELY!!!

This new world of Blue Collar skilled trades is truly that --- a new world. Construction is not the only industry which relies on these skilled trade workers. Most major companies rely on skilled workers to assemble and repair and support their product development, manufacturing and installation efforts. Blue Collar work and workers are changing. Pay is getting better and required skills are more complex. Those qualified workers are more difficult to find. In order to get a job in this workforce, you need to have a resume.

So what is a Resume? A resume is an outline of your jobs, training and education. Yes. It is that! But a resume should also be much more than that. The resume should highlight and sell the skills and abilities which YOU will use in your new job.

You need to highlight your skills and your talents (those same talents discussed in the chapter on Assessing Yourself). What do you bring to a job? A lot of the resume should be directed at what YOU want to do in your next job. What have you trained for? What are your skills and talents? What do you like to do and what are innately GOOD at doing?

Skilled trades have become more and more technically complex. There is a lot more involved in doing the work.

The economy fluctuates. You, yourself, change and find different challenges and dreams. You may find yourself out of a job, no matter what your skills and experience. So you need to understand what it takes to get another job. The rules for you have changed some. Not only have you moved into a specialized, skilled role, but these skilled trades jobs are becoming increasingly more technically complex.

Writing and presenting a good resume can be complex and requires some special skills you may not have. You may want to talk with a resume/job search expert. You should at least buy one of the good books on the subject. There are a number now for Blue Collar jobs out there. (for example, Blue Collar Resumes by Steven Provensazo and The Blue Collar Resume and Job Hunting Guide by Ron and Caryl Krannich).

Interview for the job

Preparation is the key to success in any job interview. Have you reviewed each step in the process, understand who you are, your qualifications, how your capabilities relate to this specific job. You know about your own desire and determination, your own fastidiousness and energy and drive to do a good job. Make sure the employer knows those things about you before you leave. But being aggressive during the interview is not the way to make those points. Instead, you could tell a few stories about your work 'adventures' - perhaps, just a few short incidents which will show what you have done in the past and what you can do.

Getting to this interview step may be difficult -- or you just may walk into the neighborhood plumber's shop and talk to the manager. However you get in the door, the interview is definitely the last critical step in getting the job. It can be very stressful. Your job during the interview is two fold. You need to sell yourself to this employer and you need to make sure the job is one you want. If you have done the research on the job for which you are interviewing and you know yourself -- i.e. you know something about their job and a lot about your skills, capabilities, desire and determination -- then you will be ready to do this. You need to walk away from this interview knowing that you did the best you could do. You also need to be able to review that interview later and learn from it -- to be better next time. Could you have done or said something in a different manner which might have been made a better impression? What? Could you have done or said anything which would have made you feel better about yourself and the interview?

Point number two is to get more information about the job and employer. You need to walk away from this interview knowing whether you want the job or not and what about the job is good for you. It won't hurt to let the interviewer understand that you are interested in knowing the company and the job in much the same way they are interested in knowing you.

Preparation for an interview. Knowing yourself, what your goals are, what your accomplishments have been -- those are, of course, important. However, you should not expect to just recite word for word a canned speech - like your resume in audio. You can anticipate a good 80 - 85% of the questions which will be asked. In fact, you should make sure that you offer any information which you think is important, even if you are not asked directly. Role playing with someone you trust would be a good preparation. You can laugh at yourself and each other. But seriously, that is how many of the great sales and motivation teaching is done. You need to be able to think on your feet; know the material well (which is you, your qualifications and the job); and be able to articulate clearly and thoughtfully. You should anticipate the parts of the interview process, the questions and the most probable topics and include those in your role play scenarios. You should also prepare to ask intelligent questions. Those answers should be of interest to you and you should indicate that during the interviews.

Role playing ahead of time CAN help. The more you practice, the better communication skills you will develop and the better your interview should go. If you have the facilities, videotape the role playing sessions. You will be surprised just how much you learn. And, you should throw yourself into the process and learn from it. Try it again (and again.) Do not be too down on yourself as you watch the replays. Remember that everyone feels pretty much the same shock (horror?) when they see and hear themselves for the first few times on camera. (Or maybe you will be fantastic the first time -- a natural on camera. Be sure to consider a TV career if that's the case. OK, that was supposed to be a joke.)

There is one of life's rules which you should also keep in mind during this process: Learning is a layered process. Iteration is a key. Do it once. Fail. Learn from that failure. Do it Again. (By the way -- that's one of the reasons for the role playing --- you can do it, fail, do it again, fail -- repeatedly. Without impacting an actual job situation.)

Skills you should include in your role play scenarios include both verbal and non verbal communications. What you say is critical, of course. However, how you communicate non verbally may play an even greater role in the selling of yourself process. How you dress, stand, sit, use your hands, and your facial communication notes are important in the two way communication.

Expect also, that you may be asked to return for multiple interviews and multiple interviewers. Actually, being called back is a good sign. A very good sign. Go into a second and third interview with the same enthusiasm and newness as the first.

Don't expect interviews to be just the formal, sit down across a desk situations. You may find formal or informal interviews occur over the telephone, across a doorway in a body shop, while watching someone repair an electrical outlet. Recognize the situation. Give complete, enthusiastic answers and ask the same kind of questions -- as you would prepare for a formal interview in a sit down office situation. The result could be your new job.

If you are applying for a job -- or going specifically for a requested job interview -- whatever your rationale for meeting with the interviewer -- dress appropriately for the site you are visiting. A suit and tie may be great for a formal office situation. Slacks, shirt and a blazer may be more appropriate for the job site location.

Negotiate for the pay, benefits, working conditions you need.

In some jobs, there are some recognized pay rates and definite preset scales based on experience and other factors. Find out ahead of time what the circumstances and realities are for the job, company and industry. Be ready to negotiate for the working conditions, the pay, benefits you need and expect ... during the discussions about extending the job offer. How you do that depends on the circumstances and the people involved. You do not want to get a lower offer than would be extended -- by speaking about your own requirements too soon. However, you need to make it clear if an offer is definitely lower than you can accept. You need to have thought about this ahead of time and know what your definites are: i.e. definitely no lower salary rate than ...; definitely must have health benefits for family, etc. Make sure that the employer/hiring person knows what you need in order to come to work. However, make sure that what you say and indicate are factual. Let them make the offer. Find out what range they are looking at. You probably know by now what the working conditions will be. Think about whether they are acceptable to you. Look at the pay range versus the local and national market versus what your skill level is right now. You should also try to negotiate a review time period -- i.e. take the offered rate and benefits with a guaranteed review and raise in six to nine months based on your performance. Or something similar.

Yea! You got the job offer.
Do you want the job?

OK -- first thing to do is -- Congratulate yourself. Enjoy the success. You have achieved a major accomplishment. You can learn from this positive experience.

Now -- do you want this job? Is it right for you? Ask yourself whether you should take the job. It's one thing to get the job --- it is another to make sure you ask -- do you want This Job? Is it a good job requiring the skills you have and can you learn and gain good experience... even better skills? What are the long term prospects? Do the pay and benefits give you what you need and are they competitive with the market? How about the location, the people, the job itself? Hopefully, you have negotiated a great deal and you can start next week.

Walk into your new life with joy and confidence. Take the steps to make your new life one of renewed hope and adventure.

You did it!

You made changes in your life which will make you more financially secure, happier, and more confident in your future. That takes a lot of courage, determination and passion.

Congratulations.

This book is not about how to live your life. However, here are a few ideas and pointers for living which might be worth sharing. Hopefully, you will think it worthwhile to add some of these thoughts to your own meditation list for review.

Career Expectations

Manage your new career. Do you want to advance into management. Get to be the best at your craft that you can be? Start your own company. What do you want in the short, medium and long term from your career?

Now you need to make sure you know what you expect from this new career, and this new life, you are making-for yourself. Of course, you have already thought a lot about this during the process of getting there. However, now you will experience the job for real and can make some decisions about your own satisfaction level. Are you happy about your career decisions so far? Remember, life is not just a single set of decisions. You may not want to envision this new job status as a final plateau. However, for now, you most likely will want to concentrate on making it work and enjoying your new life. You have definitely earned a period for quiet satisfaction in your achievement.

Your Busy Life:
Focus on the Critical...
Focus on YOU

What is important? You need to make the time to live your life and get the most out of the daily joys of living. If your kids have a play or dance recital, that's important. Concentrate on how you make sure the personal, family and friends, i.e. those important parts of your life, are included in your schedule. AND take the time to enjoy them.

'Oh ... RIGHT!', you say. How do I do that when work, kids' schedules, car breakdowns and all the other daily obstacles of living interfere ... *all the time.* Yes ... you can only fit in some of those things. I have a couple of things which worked for me ... with two kids, no husband, and a full time career. Here's some thoughts:

> **Find at least 30 minutes to an hour a day ... just for yourself.** Meditate, read, take a hot bath and soak or something. Just make sure you completely unwind. That not only takes having the time, it also means knowing how to totally relax. This book isn't about that ... but there are some books and programs which will show you how.

Don't walk around this need forever. I think it is like physical exercise. If you put it off too long, it becomes less and less easy to make it happen. Taking time each day for yourself, by yourself, coupled with the power to relax completely for awhile, is tremendously IMPORTANT. It is important to maintaining joy in your life, as well as, to sustaining your long term physical and emotional health.

Financial Planning

Learn the basics of financial planning and successful money management. Now is the time, when you are in a new beginning for your financial life, to review basic financial strategies for success. Just a few notes on that:
- Go find yourself a good book on personal and family finances. READ it.
- Pay yourself first. That is a cliche, and it is a cliche, because it is true and important. Now that you are making more money than ever before, take a portion of it and put it into savings and investments. Make it so that you will not, and maybe even *cannot*, change that payment to yourself. i.e. you automatically must make it.
- Pay off your credit cards as soon as you possibly can do so. Then, if you keep one or two -- pay it off monthly.

Those are just a couple of the rules for personal financial management which are going to make your life better now and in the future. Get that book, read it and follow the advice. This area of your life is worth some serious attention.

Juggling the Balls

Managing relations, kids, self, work, and any kind of social life. Each one and all are all essential parts of your life. You must figure out how to make time for them - your partner, kids, family, friends. Often that is not easy. Know how to pare down to basics. There is no easy answer, but support networks of family and friends certainly help.

Emotional Stability and Self Discipline

Say a special thanks to your support system --- friends, family -- whoever has been instrumental in making it happen for you.

Take a breath and enjoy *just living* for a little while.

> *(That's frequently the answer my sister gives me when I call to see how she is doing ... 'Just living', she says. She is 'not much of a talker', as my daughter has said, and adds 'unlike you, Mom'. So, that answer has become both funny and sometimes infuriating. But I do know what she means.)* Take some of your new 'sort of' *more available?* time to talk with your sister (or your mother, brother, aunt or whoever you are close to) if you feel like it.

Entrench yourself in the new routines, the new feelings of freedom and achievement. Enjoy those achievements.

You have found out just how difficult changing your life can be if you have gone through a career change process. In just living your *normal, packed full of life*, life, you know to expect complexities and difficulty. Keeping an emotional equilibrium is sometimes difficult.

If we are normal, then we know to expect occasional depression. That's not unusual. Everyone gets depressed. You just learn to turn your mind back to hope, planning, and good and productive subjects. People, family, hope for the future, specific plans for your children, your avocations (like painting? or more) can pull you out of the morass. Mental tricks which patch humor onto your unique life videos sometimes work. Whatever works for you is good. You may find, also, that you need to allow yourself a few hours of down/depression time. My statement to my family is 'I'm going into my corner and eat a few worms.' Do that or close to it. I allow myself the time to be depressed. I think a little bout of depression, like the physical act of crying, can be cathartic. The trick is to make sure to come out fighting and laughing. (Pick a fight with an understanding family member or your partner. I find that helps, sometimes. OK, Sis, don't read this part.)

Of course, it is OK to re-assess the decisions you have made ---- the goals you have achieved or not achieved yet. That is thoroughly human. It is also human to begin setting your own new goals. But - take some time to enjoy where you are -- who you are becoming.

Life is good.

Enjoy it.

Go For It, Girlfriend!

& Don't Forget

Click in
to
www.BlueCollarWoman.com

AND

**TELL US
HOW
YOU
ARE
DOING?**

Independent Women with Confidence

BLUE COLLAR WOMAN®
Yes We Can!

APPENDICES

A. SUPPORT ORGANIZATIONS FOR WOMEN

B. RESEARCH TIPS

C. PERSONALITY TYPES & CAREERS

D. APPRENTICESHIPS & TECHNICAL SCHOOLS

E. Career Information Example: CARPENTERS

Independent Women with Confidence

A. Support Organizations for Women

There are support organizations to help women get into skilled trades and these organization will be there for those women during the process and career transition. The number of these organizations has been growing. Check out also the union administration and websites. Frequently, there are embedded units to assist women. Make sure that these embedded support groups are part of your first research and contact points. They can help.

There are also groups like the Chicago Women in Trade, National Organization for Women in Trades. You will find groups in your local geographic area. Look for them on the web and through your local community colleges and contractor groups.

Make contact with them and follow their advice. Here are a few -- Find some in your local area and make sure you contact them. They can advise and help.

TRADES ORGANIZATIONS for Women
Organizations working toward equity in the building and construction trades.

Chicago Women in Trades
Chicago Women in Trades works to increase the number of women in the skilled trades and other blue collar occupations and to eliminate the barriers that prohibit women from entering and remaining in non-traditional careers.

Hard Hatted Women
Hard Hatted Women is a dedicated to promoting women's economic empowerment by ensuring equal access and opportunity to all jobs, especially non-traditional.

Nontraditional Employment for Women (NEW)
NEW is a nonprofit organization dedicated to helping low-income women find economic self-sufficiency through work in the blue-collar trades. NEW is located in New York City.

Sisters in the Building Trades
A Washington-based group supporting women in the building trades through networking, outreach to the community (speakers' bureau) and mentorship.

Tradeswomen, Inc.
Tradeswomen, Inc. is a non-profit grass roots organization whose purpose is to promote and support women in non-traditional blue collar jobs. Founded in 1979, they are based in the San Francisco Bay Area. Tradeswomen, Inc. has three goals:
• Recruit more women into building and construction trades.
• Promote retention of women in the trades
• Develop tradeswomen's capacity for leadership and career growth, on the job and in their unions

Washington Women in Trades
The Washington Women in Trades produces the annual Women in Trades Fair in Seattle.
Women in Construction Company

WICC is a women-owned construction company that is a subsidiary of a non-profit women's organization. They recruit and train low-income women who want to learn construction skills and earn living wages.

West Virginia Women Work
- West Virginia Women Work is a statewide non-profit organization that supports and advocates for the education, employment and economic equity for all women. We achieve this goal through a comprehensive program of recruitment, training, referrals, placements, networking, advocacy, retention activities and public workshops.
- While the nonprofit's headquarters is in Morgantown, there are presently three active skilled trades training sites (Step-Up for Women) located in the state – North Central West Virginia (Morgantown), the Eastern Panhandle (Martinsburg) and Kanawha Valley (Charleston). This program boasts an 80% job placement rate with new graduates earning a minimum of $3 more per hour than a traditional job.

Women Unlimited
Women Unlimited improves the economic well-being of Maine women, minorities, and displaced workers by providing access to, and support in, trade, technical, and transportation careers.

Oregon Tradeswomen, Inc.
3934 NE Martin Luther King Jr. Boulevard, Suite 101
Portland, OR 97212

Here are a few more links for you -- more about those for women and others who can and want to help.

9 to 5 National Association of Working Women

AFL-CIO Women's Department
Blue Collar Gal
Chicago Women in Trades
Coalition of Labor Union Women (CLUW)
Electrical Workers Local Union 6 (San Francisco)
Equal Rights Advocates
Hard Hatted Women (Cleveland)
Home Builders Institute
Ironworking.com
National Association of Women in Construction
National Partnership for Women and Families
National Women's History Project
Non-traditional Employment for Women (NYC)
Oregon Tradeswomen
Pride and a Paycheck
Rosie the Riveter Memorial (Richmond, CA)
Sisters in the Building Trades
Solar Energy International (workshops for women)
State Building and Construction Trades Council (California)
The Women's Bureau - U.S. Dept. of Labor
Tradeswomen Now and Tomorrow
Vermont Works for Women
Washington Women in Trades
Women In Overalls (Chat Group)
Women's Labor History
Work for Women

Appendix B
Research Tips

The Largest Search Engines are probably

Google, Yahoo!, Bing

A few more are: MSN Live, Ask, AOL Search

Search Engines index different pages and have different capabilities. You may want to use more than one to find what you are looking for.

Advanced Commands
Use the Advanced commands of the Search Engines. You can save lots of time and almost always find more information which will be helpful.

Search Engine Results (advanced commands are compiled by automated robots that search for and index web pages.)
    These might help for more specifics.
Google Advanced search help; Google Advanced page.
Yahoo! Advanced search; Yahoo! shortcuts and More Yahoo! shortcuts
Bing Advanced (formerly Live search) search options
Ask Search Tips and Ask Advanced search
Gigablast Advanced search

Worth taking a look:
Web Searching Tips at *Search Engine Watch*
Choose the Best Search Engine for Your...(search) from *Noodle Tools*
Best Search Tools Chart from *InfoPeople*
Pandia All-in-One List for Search Engines and Directories

Appendix C
Personality Types
& Careers

> Our thanks for the information in this appendix to the people at www.personalitypage.com. Go take a look at their site. Good stuff!

Personality types have been shown to have some relationship to career choices and to career success. It is certainly good to know about personality types and also to know what the research appears to have shown about these career to personality type relationships. Do not take this information as your primary and sole guide in the selection of a career. You are making some excellent choices if you decide to take some of the personality tests and find out more about your 'personality type'. The career information included here is just a sample. *Most of it is from the www.personalitypage.com.* Go take a look and check out more of their great website.

However, keep in mind -- you must make your own decisions. Tests and theories are great. But what does your gut (for want of another term) say to you about yourself. What do you really want to do -- what is your d'ruthers choice. Listen to your SELF, your wants, your cares, your innate abilities. Know the information and know what you can about yourself -- then make your decision based - not on tests and experts -- but on your own self knowledge.

Here's the list of the Personality Types we discussed in the chapter on Assess Yourself.

- ISTJ - Internal/Sensing/Thinking/Judging
- ESTJ - External/Sensing/Thinking/Judging
- ISFJ - Internal/Sensing/Feeling/Judging (Nur-

turers)
- ESFJ - External/Sensing/Feeling/Judging (Caregivers)
- ISTP - Internal/Sensing/Thinking/Perceiving (Mechanics)
- ESTP - External/Sensing/Thinking/Perceiving (Doers)
- ESFP - External/Sensing/Feeling/Perceiving (Performers)
- ISFP - Internal/Sensing/Feeling/Perceiving (Artists)
- ENTJ - External/Intuitive/Thinking/Judging (Executives)
- INTJ - Internal/Intuitive/Thinking/Judging (Scientists)
- ENTP - External/Intuitive/Thinking/Perceiving (Visionaries)
- INTP - Internal/Intuitive/Thinking/Perceiving (Thinkers)
- ENFJ - External/Intuitive/Feeling/Judging (Givers)
- ENFP - External/Intuitive/Feeling/Perceiving (Inspirers)
- INFP - Internal/Intuitive/Feeling/Perceiving (Idealists)

Career Choices for Personality Types

(The information which follows is from www.personalitypage.com. For lot's more information -- go check out their website. Good Stuff!)

Understanding your own strengths and weaknesses is important in selecting a successful career which you can and will enjoy. Knowing the personality traits which you believe that are part of you is a good first step. A good next step is to know what the researchers have discovered about the known, defined personality types and successful career choices have been for people which have been tested as specific personality types. Here is some of that information for you to mull over. (I say again --- take it all with a grain of sand. Use it to analyze yourself -- for yourself -- to know you better. If it makes sense and feels right -- use it.)

Another note here ---- check out some of the blogs on the internet which include people who are already in the Blue Collar Skilled Trades -- and find out what personality type they think they are. Interesting!!! Just another FYI --- they range all over the place.

ISTJ

ISTJs persevere -- and feel they can do almost anything that they have decided to do. An ISTJ will do best in a career in which they can use their excellent organizational skills and their powers of concentration to create order and structure. They seem to fit well into management.

Here are some possible career paths for the ISTJ:

- Business executives, administrators, managers
- Accountants, financial officers
- Police and detectives
- Judges
- Lawyers
- Medical Doctors/ Dentists
- Computer Programmers, systems analyssts, computer scientists
- Military leaders

ESTJ

ESTJs have a lot of flexibility in types of careers - since they are good at a lot of different things. They spend a lot of effort in doing things the right way. Happiest in leaderhip positions -- they have natural drive to be in charge. Best suited for jobs which reuire creating order and structure.

Here are some possible career paths for the ESTJ:

- Military leaders
- Business administrators and managers

Independent Women with Confidence

- Police, detectives
- Judges
- Financial officers
- Teachers
- Sales Representatives

ISFJ

ISFJs are very interested and 'in tune' with how other people are feeling. They enjoy creating structure and order and very good at it. They are best in a career where they can use their exceptional people/observation skills to determine what people want or need, and then use their organizational abilities to create a structured plan/environment for achieving what people want. Their excellent sense of space and function combined with their awareness of aesthiteic quality also gives them quite special abilities in the more artistic endeavors, such as interior decorating and clothes design.

Here are some possible career paths for the ISFJ:

- Interior decorators
- Designers
- Nurses
- Administrators and managers
- Administrative Assistants
- Child Care
- Social Work / counselors
- Paralegals
- Clergy / Religious Worker
- Office managers
- Shopkeepers
- Bookkeepers
- Home Economists

ESFJ

ISTJs persevere -- and feel they can do almost anything that they have decided to do. An ISTJ will do best in a career in which they can use their excellent organizational skills and their powers of concentration to create order and structure. They seem to fit well into management.

Here are some possible career paths for the ISTJ:

- Business executives, administrators, managers
- Accountants, financial officers
- Police and detectives
- Judges
- Lawyers
- Medical Doctors/ Dentists
- Computer Programmers, systems analyssts, computer scientists
- Military leaders
- Office managers
- Shopkeepers
- Bookkepers
- Home Economics

ISTP

ISTP's are good at multiple tasks. Introverted and like autonomy - not lots of structructure. Like working for themselves and/or in flexible environments.

Here are some possible career paths for the ISTP:

- Police and detective
- Forensic Pathologists
- Cmputer Programmers, System Anslysts, Computer Specialists
- Engineers
- Carpenters
- Mechanics
- Pilots, Drivers, Motorcyclists
- Athletes
- Entrepreneurs

ESTP

Skills of observation -- good at analyzing and assessing other people. Good people skills. React uickly and effectively to immediate needs.

Here are some possible career paths for the ESTP:

- Sales

Independent Women with Confidence

- Marketing
- Police
- Paramedic/Emergency Medical Tech
- PC technicians
- Computer Technical Support
- Entrepreneurs

ESFP

Lots of skills. Need contact with people and new experiences. Choose careers which provide opportunity to use people skills and practical perspective - along with new challenges.

Here are some possible career paths for the ESFP:

- Artists, performers, actors
- Sales
- Counselors/Social work
- Child care
- Fashion Designers
- Interior decorators
- Consultants
- Photographers

ISFP

Strong core of inner values - prefer to live in the moment - need space and freedom - Very aware of people's feelings and reactions, driven by innter values to help people.

Here are some possible career paths for the ISFP

- Artist
- Musician/composer
- Designer
- Child care
- Social Worker/Counselor
- Teacher
- Psychologist
- Veterinarian
- Forest Ranger
- Pediatrician

ENTJ
Leaders and organization builders. Ability to identify problems and solutions. Strong desire to lead. Likes to be in charge.

Here are some possible career paths for the ENTJ:

- Corporate Executive Office
- Entrepreneur
- Computer Consultant
- Lawyer
- Judge
- Business Administrators
- University Professors/Administrators

INTJ
Can grasp complex theories and apply to problems and long term strategies. Need autonomy over daily life.

Here are some possible career paths for the ESTP:

- Scientists
- Engineers
- Professors/Teachers
- Medical Doctors/Dentists
- Corporate Strategists
- Business Administrators/Managers
- Military Leaders
- Lawyers
- Judges
- Computer Programmers, Analysts, Specialists

ENTP
Wide range of capabilities. Generally good at anything which captures thier interest.

Here are some possible career paths for the ENTP:

- Lawyers
- Psychologists
- Entrepreneurs
- Photographers
- Consultants

- Engineers
- Scientists
- Actors
- Sales
- Marketing
- Computer Programmers, Analysts, Specialists

INTP

Special gift with generating and analyzing theories; insight and are creative thinkers - can grasp abstract thoughts. Logical and rational reasoning skills.

Here are some possible career paths for the INTP:

- Scientist
- Photographers
- Strategic Planners
- Mathematicians
- University Professors
- Computer Programmers, analysts, specialists
- Technical Writers
- Engineers
- Lawyers
- Judges
- Forensic Research
- Forestry/Park Rangers

ENFJ

Interested in people. Value other's feelings, want structure and organization. Creative and imaginative. Personal satisfaction from helping others. Sensitive to discord. Need approval from others.

Here are some possible career paths for the ENFJ:

- Faciliator
- Consultant
- Psychologist
- Social Worker
- Teacher
- Clergy

- Sales
- Human Resources
- Manager
- Events coordinator
- Politicians
- Writers

D. Apprenticeships & Technical Schools

Apprenticeships
So -- what do you need to know about Apprenticeships?

What are Apprenticeships: Apprenticeships are government regulated, sponsored programs which offer formal, structured education and on-the-job hands-on skilled trades learning, i.e. classroom instruction combined with on-the-job training. There are about 140 skilled trades with formal apprenticeships available. Depending on your choice, the apprenticeship can take two to five years to complete.

Earn as you Learn... ... Apprentices learn occupational skills in the classroom, and that learning is expanded to include hands-on, paid, on-the-job training. Students learn and practice all phases of the trade/occupation in real-world applications. You will spend probably 8-10 weeks of each year in formal in class education and the remainder of the time on the job. *Registered Apprenticeship* is a training strategy that pays wages to apprentices from the first day of their apprenticeship. These wages are a portion of the skilled wage rate which usually increases throughout the training program. The wage, along with every other aspect of the apprentice-

Job	Average Annual Pay	Annual Openings
Electricians	$41,680	65,000
Pipefitters	40,950	56,000
Plumbers	41,000	56,000
Heating/Air Conditions Mechs	35,560	35,000
Refrigeration Mechs	35,560	35,000
Sheet metal workers	35,000	30,000
Brick Masons	41,550	21,000
Telecommunications line installers	39,540	13,000
Carpenters (Assemblers/Rpr)	34,250	193,000
Carpenters (Rough)	34,250	193,000
Carpenters (Framing)	34,250	193,000

Here are just a few of the careers which may be entered through apprenticeships. These are some of the typical salaries and number of jobs available (in 2007) according to the US Department of Labor.

ship program, is provided for, regulated and monitored by federal and local government agencies along with employers and educators.

You will need to be accepted into an apprenticeship program. That may be through a union or independent group. You may need to pay tuition fees for the in-school portion of the apprenticeship. However, in most cases of licensed apprenticeship programs this is paid for you. In many cases these are set up with local community or technical colleges.

Apprenticeship Programs are available in most states. If there is no State licensing and regulatory board -- there are federal and perhaps local organizations which provide the sponsorship. Local community colleges and local employers are good places to contact for information. And -- as always --- check the internet for skilled trades apprenticeship programs in your local geographical area. Check the specific union websites, since they are the most likely source and sponsor of apprenticeship programs. There may be dates and places to go for application and testing.

www.CALApprenticeship.org is the california website for apprenticeship information. This website (www.calapprenticeship.org) provides information and names and links to various skilled trades programs and links in California. You should be able to find something similar with information in your state. If not, go to the Federal Labor websites to research your area.

Portable Credentials

A Registered Apprenticeship is a training program which is covered by a legal agreement (contract). Apprentices receive a Certificate of Qualification in the chosen trade, i.e. the registered apprenticeship program leads to a certificate of completion and you leave (graduate) the program with a status of skilled journey level specialist (journeywoman). You are recognized as a skilled trades expert. Certification for the apprenticeship program in California is sponsored by the California Division of Apprenticeship Standards (DAS). As they emphasize, the credentials have explicit meaning, recognition, and respect in the eyes of federal and state governments and relevant industries and employers. More than twenty states have such a division/organization for apprenticeship programs. If there is no state organization or recognition in your state, the credentials will be federally sponsored.

Apprenticeship leads to ...

Apprenticeship programs train people to become recognized competent skilled trades specialists. (usually called journeyman/journeywoman.) Apprenticeships are a great foundation for any career in the skilled trades. You get the education, the training and develop the skill sets which translate into competency and knowledge necessary for your chosen skilled trade career. Apprentice 'graduates' are recognized as having the capabilities to 'do the job' across the industry.

The California Trades Group which sponsors apprenticeships says it this way:

> By participating in a program, local apprenticeship training committees shape applicants with character, aptitude, motivation and good personality traits into competent journeymen and journeywomen who have in-demand skill sets, comprehensive knowledge, positive attitudes and superior abilities.

History of Apprenticeship

There has been a very long history of apprenticeships ... ... at least back through the middle ages. In current history, a major milestone in the United States was the Fitzgerald act of 1937. This established a national advisory committee to draft regulations for apprenticeship programs. Later, the Act was amended to assign the United States Department of Labor the authority to issue regulations protecting health, safety and general welfare of apprentices. Those laws also emphasized a very important aspect of the apprenticeship programs -- the use of contracts in the hiring and employment of the apprentices. The Apprenticeship program, based on the Fitzgerald Act, is administered by the Employment and Training Administration in the Department of Labor. The Apprenticeship regulations are included in the US Code of Federal Regulations. This is also where the regulations banning racial, ethnic, religious, age and gender discrimination in apprenticeship programs are located. These labor standards (under Title 29 CFR Part 29) set out the policies and procedures to promote equality of opportunity in apprenticeship programs registered with the US Department of Labor and in state apprenticeship programs registered with recognized state apprenticeship agencies. (How well this is actually happening for women is still open to question. My research shows 'not so great' so far.)

Essentially, what this all means, is that apprenticeship programs are registered with State and National Labor Department related agencies. There are regulations which cover such issues as formal contracts, recruitment and selection of apprentices, and all conditions of employment and training during the apprenticeships.

The National Apprenticeship Laws were expected to 'extend the application of apprenticeship standards by encouraging the inclusion of contracts of apprenticeship, to bring together employers and labor for the formulation of programs of apprenticeship, to cooperate with State agencies in the formulation of standards of apprenticeship.' The Fitzgerald Act of 1937 laid the groundwork for today's system of Federal Government regulations and assistance in apprenticeship programs. Now there is a Bureau of Apprenticeship and Training, which includes representation of employers and labor, plus representatives of the US Office of Education. This Bureau of Apprenticeship and Training is the national administrative agency in the Department of Labor which carries out the objectives of the Apprenticeship law. The Agency is guided by the recommendations of the Federal Committee on Apprenticeship. The Bureau works closely with employer and labor groups, vocational schools, and state apprenticeship programs. The Bureau develops and disseminates apprenticeship information through newspapers, industrial periodicals, discussions at annual conventions of employer associations and unions and regional apprenticeship conferences.

Apprenticeship Programs

So what does all this history and information about the laws and National and State involvement in Apprenticeship Programs mean to you?

Guarantees

There are hundreds of apprenticeable occupations which are covered in registered programs. Most of these are in the construction, manufacturing, transportation and service industries. If you are accepted into one of these apprenticeship programs, then you can know that your schools and training will be of value and provide you with the basics to get a job in your chosen career. These guarantees include the following aspects of your apprenticeship:

Paid School and Training;

National recognition as a skilled crafts journeyman/journeywoman when completed. This includes:

- Program subject matter and included topics of study and training.
- Cross transference of the training.

- Pay rates, times and benefits.
- Structured programs which are laid out up front - so you can plan for the program requirements.
- Starting age -- 16 plus.
- Full and fair opportunity to all to apply for apprenticeship.
- Schedule of work processes in which an apprentice is to receive training and experience on the job.
- Program includes organized instruction designed to provide apprentices with knowledge and technical subjects related to their trade (a minimum of 144 hours per year is normally considered necessary).
- Progressively increasing schedule of wage.
- Proper supervision of on-the-job training with adequate facilities to train apprentices.
- Apprentice progress, both in job performance and related instruction, is evaluated periodically and appropriate records are maintained.
- Employee/employer cooperation.
- Successful completions are recognized.
- No discrimination in any phase of selection, employment or training.

For those who are Just starting out --- you can:
- Earn as learn,
- When completed, you can be assured of a secure future and a good standard of living because the training is in a craft where skills are much in demand.
- Opportunities for employment and advancement open up with the recognition that the apprentices are now skilled craft workers.

Certifications of Completion

When apprentices finish their training, they receive certificates of completion of apprenticeship. These are issued by the state apprenticeship agencies or, in those States not having such an agency, by the Federal Bureau of Apprenticeship and Training, in accordance with its recommended standards.

Joint Apprenticeship Committees

There are Joint Apprenticeship Committees which are composed of representatives of management and labor. These committees work together to develop and administer local apprenticeship training programs. There are also national trade committees which represent national organizations. The national committees formulate policies on apprenticeship in the various trades and issue basic standards to be used by affiliated organization.

Basic Apprenticeship Standards and Requirements

How do you get to be an apprentice? What are the requirements?

Minimum Requirements: Apprenticeship basic qualifications vary from one trade to another --- but most require the following basics:

- a high school diploma or General Equivalency Diploma (GED)
- transportation (to and from work)
- must be physically able to do the work
- must have ability to work with your hands

Other requirements are:
- specified math skills
- completion of certain courses, like applied English, drafting, chemistry, algebra and geometry, industrial arts
- may need ability to work at elevated heights or other such special requirements

Reality Requirements: Getting into an apprenticeship program can be very competitive. You need to study the particular trade and apprenticeship program of interest to you. Contact them and find out, first hand, what the requirements are and what the competition is. One of the apprenticeship contacts in Georgia told me that the preliminary tests are very stiff. Their preliminary tests were in math and English. Can you realistically expect to get one of the apprenticeships? Can you work towards getting more of the basic requirements and then expect to enter the program? If the apprenticeship is through a union, find out who gets the apprenticeship opportunities. Is there a pattern to the selected candidates?

Finding Apprenticeship Programs

You can find local Apprenticeship Programs with a quick search on the internet using the key words, skilled trades and Apprenticeships/Apprenticeship programs. You can also contact the US Department of Labor, Bureau of Apprenticeship and Training -- either the national website and offices -- or check out state listings. For example, in Illinois, the Bureau of Apprenticeship and Training is listed in Rockford, Il., and there is an Area Training Representative with a listed telephone number -- as part of the website which lists some of the trades offering apprenticeship programs. Most states have a similar website and local contact information.

Some of the listings for apprenticeship programs, for example, in Illinois are:

> Bricklayers Local; Iron Workers Local; Dist Carpenters; Laborers Training Program; Painters and Allied Trades; Northern Illinois Electrical; Electricians Local; Plasters and Cement Masons Local; Plumbers and Pipefitters Local; Roofing Systems; Rockford Training and Machining Association; Roofers Local; Sheet Metal Workers Local; Operating Engineers

> These are just a few of the trade groups and unions offering apprenticeship programs in one part of Illinois.

More About: How to become an Apprentice

Here is how the apprenticeship program website for the state of Washington describes the process for applying for an apprenticeship program:

> *If you are sure you are ready to apply, then the simplest method to find a program and apply is as follows:*

1. Go to the webpage registered apprenticeship programs by county. The Acrobat (PDF) files on this page are sorted by County and then by occupation and list all registered apprenticeship programs that cover that county.
2. Download the file(s) that you want to review.
3. Review the files and when you find a occupation or occupations that you would like to apply for, contact the Program directly using the contact information provided, to find out if the program is taking applications.
4. If the program is taking applications, then you follow their procedures for applying.

Note: The Acrobat files on the webpage are updated only about monthly. To run a "current" county listing, you need to go to our public online "Apprenticeship Registration and Tracking System" web page and run the report "Find an Apprenticeship Program by County," then follow Number 2, 3, and 4.
===
o   In Washington State: Use our online Apprenticeship Registration and Tracking System (ARTS) database and look for registered apprenticeship programs by: :
o   By county – Print a report of those apprenticeship programs available in the county where you plan on living and working. (Recommended Method)
or
o   By occupation – Print a report of those apprenticeship programs that provide training in the occupation you are interested in.
o   Registered apprenticeship programs by county with occupations and contact information. These are pre-made Acrobat files for each county which are sorted by occupation and list all registered apprenticeship programs that cover that county. Includes appropriate contact information.

o   In other states: You may also go to the following websites for information on apprenticeship programs governed by the Federal Government or in other states.
o   Career Voyages.
o   Apprenticeship Training, Employer and Labor Services (OATELS).

These sites list apprenticeship program sponsors recognized and registered by the federal Office of Apprenticeship Training, Employer and Labor Services (OATELS) or other State Registration agencies (where appropriate).

Review the Apprenticeship Program Standards for the program(s) you want to apply for... so that you have a good understanding of what you will be doing and what will be required of you. Go to Apprenticeship Program Standards Web page. These are the documents that the Apprenticeship Programs use to run their programs.

o   Once you have decided on a specific apprenticeship program, here's what you need to do...
o   Contact the program directly.
o   Ask if they are taking applications.
o   Follow their instructions for applying.

If you are accepted into a registered apprenticeship program...

...the program sponsor will send in your registration information to the Apprenticeship Central Office, which will register you as a Washington State Apprentice. You will then receive a registration card.

NOTE: Some registered apprenticeships (electrical, plumbing, dispensing optician) also require that you apply for a Trainee card or other license. Please check with your apprenticeship program about any additional license requirements.

For more information

If you have any questions or concerns, or if you need paper copies of any of these documents, please contact:
- *the Apprenticeship Coordinator for your area or*
- *the Central Apprenticeship Office*

Technical Schools and Community Colleges

So -- what do you need to know about Technical Schools and Community Colleges?

What are they?

There are *not for profit* institutions and *for profit* institutions. Let's talk about the *For Profits* first. These are definitely businesses and in the game for the money. There is absolutely nothing wrong with this and it is great that there is such a wide variety of opportunities for education out there. However, for you, the potential student -- if you can find a good education product for less money, then it is only wise to do so. There is some excellent education and training to be found in the 'for profit' institutions. I have discussed some of the pitfalls earlier in this chapter.

Not for Profits, The rest of this section will be about these great *not for profit,* locally supported institutions. These are the places where you can find training and formal education post high school. Most require a High School diploma. If you don't have one, these schools will help you get an equivalency for that high school degree. They are state and locally supported, usually and may even be part of the public education system. The tuition and fees are comparatively low ... ... and there are scholarships and financial help available... with counselors to guide you through the process.

Here's part of the web page again with the fee structure of the North Ga Technology School (June/2011):

Tuition and Fees
2011-2012 Academic Year

TUITION

Standard Tuition Programs		Non-Standard Tuition Program	
$75/credit hour	GA residents	$125/ credit hour	Commercial Truck Driving
$150/credit hour	Out-of-state students		Plus $130 fuel surcharge
$300/credit hour	International students		

FEES

Fees Due Each Term Upon Registration

- $6 Accident Insurance
- $10 Athletic
- $55 Instruction/Technology
- $10 Parking
- $39 Registration
- $38 Student Activity

Fees are no longer eligible for HOPE payment

Some of the other interesting and important information about these schools for you are:

- Close ties to the local employer base. The schools usually have people whose job it is to build those ties and to ensure that their graduates are both prepared and introduced to the local employers. They manage the job process and help you get your 'foot in the door'.
- Programs are carefully crafted to meet the needs of those employers and to help you get the job when you finish.
- Apprenticeship programs. In many cases these schools provide the inclass schooling portion of local apprenticeship programs. In the case of the apprenticeships, you will have to meet the requirements for that apprenticeship program and come to the school through application and acceptance into the apprenticeship program.
- Fee structures are most likely the lowest you will find in your area. There is frequently support from local government and school systems - so you are getting, essentially, subsidized education.
- There is usually a school near where you live, e.g. in Georgia, there are twenty six institutions in the technical school system.
- They offer customized training programs for employers and for you. There is online training and the timing of the classes is usually designed for working people.
- There are frequently special programs and counseling for people who are changing careers, have lost a job, or have other circumstances which may require retraining for the job market.
- When you research these schools, you will find full and informative websites, including fee structures and help available.

Here's some of the programs available at one of the Technical Schools in the Georgia Technical Schools System. There are twenty six of these schools in the Georgia system.

Accounting
Air Conditioning Technology
Automotive
Business Administration Technology
Business Management
Certified Technical Certificates of Credit
Commercial Truck Driving
Computer Information Systems
Cosmetology
Criminal Justice
Culinary Arts
Drafting
Electrical Construction
Electrical Lineworker Apprentice
Emergency Services
Environmental Technology
Health Sciences
Horticulture
Industrial Systems Technology
Machine Tool Technology
Marine Engine Technology
Massage Therapy
Motorcycle Service Technology
Photography
Technical Communications
Turf and Golf Course Management
Welding

You can find all the schools and available training in your geographical and skilled trades area easily on the internet.

Appendix E. Some Basic Career Information-

An Example:

CARPENTERS

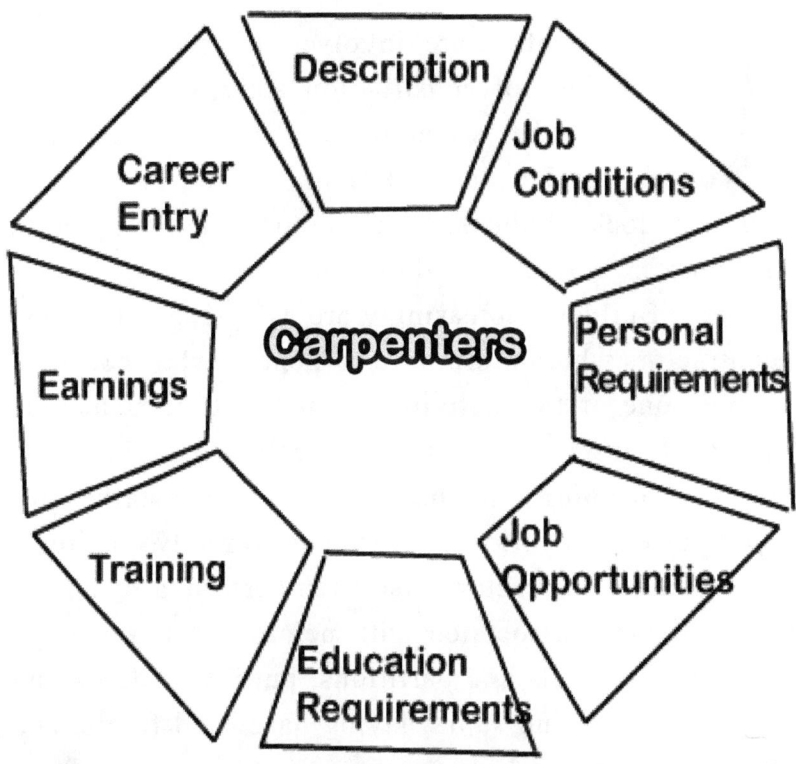

Carpenters

Description

About 30 percent of all carpenters, are self employed. Carpenters are the largest construction trade group in recent years. Many work for subcontractors and contractors in the construction industry. (Much of this information comes directly from Canadien and USA government sources.)

Carpenters are involved in many different kinds of construction activity. They cut, fit, and assemble wood and other materials for the construction of buildings, highways, bridges, docks, industrial plants, boats and many other structures. Carpenters' duties vary by the type of employer. Builders increasingly are using specialty trade contractors who, in turn, hire carpenters who specialize in just one or two activities. Such activities include setting forms for concrete construction, erecting scaffolding, or doing finishing work, such as installing interior or exterior trim. A carpenter directly employed by a general contractor must often perform a wider variety of tasks associated with new construction ... ... i.e. framing walls and partitions, putting in doors and windows, building stairs, laying hardwood floors, and hanging kitchen cabinets.

Carpenters may also be involved in any number of other tasks, e.g. build furniture, repair furniture, replace glass, and install machinery.

General carpenters construct, erect, install, maintain and repair structures and components of structures made of wood, wood-substitutes and other materials

Finish carpenters do detailed work requiring a high level of skill. Rough carpenters do framing and forming which require different and perhaps less complex skills.

Carpenters read and interpret blueprints, drawings and sketches to determine specifications and calculate requirements. Prepare layouts in conformance to building codes, using measuring tools. Measure, cut, shape, assemble and join materials. Build foundations, install floor beams, lay sub flooring and erect walls and roof systems. Fit and install trim items such as doors, stairs, moulding and hardware.

Job Conditions

The work is sometimes strenuous. There can be long periods of time in standing bending, kneeling. Carpenters work with sharp and other objects which could be dangerous if used inappropriately or in case of accidents. You may be working different projects and different bosses with frequent changing of jobs.

You could be working just about anywhere in just about any conditions -- cramped areas, heights, basements, outside, wherever.

Personal Requirements

Carpenters must have good hand/eye coordination and manual dexterity. They must be able to solve math/arithmetic problems quickly and understand basic math, reading of blueprints, and rules and building codes. A carpenter must also be physically fit in order to move around in the construction site and perform the tasks assigned. To enter an apprenticeship program, the usual minimum age is 18 and in many cases you must pass an aptitude test. You use your math skills in this trade.

You need to have the stamina to be on your feet for long periods of time. You need to be in good physical condition and able to carry your tools and materials.

Job Opportunities

The general outlook for carpenters is excellent. Economic fluctuations usually impact those in the construction industry more directly. However, because of increasing needs due to infrastructure and the aging and retirement of those currently in the job force, the need for skilled carpenters should be steady to excellent. Some of the need for carpenters will be offset by the growing use of prefabricated materials, such as pre-hung doors and windows. Carpenters can experience periods of unemployment due to the short term nature of many construction projects and the cyclical nature of the construction industry. Building can depend on many factors -- such as interest rates, economic condition, availability of building funds.

Education/Training Requirements

A high school education is desirable and should, if possible, include courses in basic math, shop, mechanical drawing and carpentry. On the job training and formal training programs are the usual methods of entry into the field. Many take vocational education courses and work informally under other skilled workers and learn that way. However, the most desirable entry is through an apprenticeship. Apprenticeships may be offered and administered through union/management or independent associations/management. For example, the United Brotherhood of Carpenters, Joiners of America, Associated General Contractors, National Association of Home Builders in the USA. In addition, training programs may be administered by local chapters of the Associated Builders and Contractors and other interested groups.

Earnings

In 2002, the median hourly earnings of carpenters was $16.44. The middle fifty percent earned $12.59 to 21.99. The highest paid were earning almost $30 per hour. Some of the more current data shows that the rate is closer to $14/hour to $33.50/hour, excluding overtime and benefits.

Career Entry

Most employers recommend entry through apprenticeship. There is sometimes stiff competition for some of these apprenticeships - so the better prepared you can be, of course, the better chance you will have. Other routes are through *on the job* training and a combination of vocational training/community college technical school and *on the job* training. It can take a good four to five years to complete an apprenticeship and become a journey level carpenter.

www.ingramcontent.com/pod-product-compliance
Lightning Source LLC
Chambersburg PA
CBHW061635040426
42446CB00010B/1422